COME UP TO THIS MOUNTAIN

Come up to this mountain

The miracle of Clarence W. Jones
& HCJB *by Lois Neely*

Tyndale House Publishers, Inc. Wheaton, Illinois

131987

Scripture references are taken
from the King James Version of the Bible.

Library of Congress Catalog Card Number 80-52237
ISBN 0-8423-0418-5
Copyright © 1980 by the World Radio Missionary Fellowship
All rights reserved
First printing, November 1980
Printed in the United States of America

Climbing is not always going forward;
Sometimes it's going sideways,
Looking for a better way
To climb the mountain.

C. W. Jones

FOREWORD

Amy Carmichael prayed, "Make us Thy mountaineers." This biography, *Come Up to This Mountain*, tells the story of God's mountaineer, Clarence W. Jones. During the more than thirty years he and I have worked together in Heralding Christ Jesus' Blessings, I've thanked God for the many fine qualities that have marked Clarence's service and person:

1. *Pioneering*. Invariably, people who know him speak of Clarence Jones's vision. He has the spirit of a pioneer. He does not look backward. He calls us to press forward. His favorite verse dramatically underscores this: "Call unto me, and I will answer thee, and shew thee great and mighty things, which thou knowest not" (Jeremiah 33:3).

2. *Perseverance*. This mountaineer has demonstrated an unswerving commitment to missionary radio. The awesome obstacles he encountered might have discouraged most of us. But once C. W. Jones heard God's call to this service he never turned back. In his appointed task he has been steadfast and unmoveable by God's grace.

3. *Principles*. Association with C. W. Jones brings inspiration. He has a refreshing directness and honesty. He hews to the line of God's revealed will. The word "straightshooter" is an apt description.

8

4. *Perspective.* Many of us have a nearsighted outlook—my work, my church, my family, my needs and opportunities. Jesus calls us to a larger perspective, to have a view of his worldwide program, to be concerned with the welfare of the whole body. A victory on one front is a victory for the whole army. C. W. Jones always keeps the larger picture in mind. He has led us in thanking God for every advance in missionary broadcasting around the world. He has always reminded us of the Lord of the Harvest's total plan.

I know you will profit from mountaineering with C. W. Jones. You will praise God as you go through the valleys and up to the heights.

We are indebted to Lois Neely for this excellent account of C. W. Jones—"Mr. Missionary Broadcaster."

Abe C. Van Der Puy
May 17, 1980

You quickly learn
in the Andes
that there are
more valleys
than mountain peaks.
C. W. Jones

INTRODUCTION

. . . *May 1933.* Clarence Jones is alone in a toolshed at the bottom of the garden in Quito, Ecuador, as clouds swirl about the peaks encircling the city. Determined to meet God, he'd come here just after daybreak. But for Clarence it was darkest night. Following the Wall Street Crash, all financial support had petered out. Now there was no money for the rent or to buy food for Katherine and the three children, let alone anything left to pay the $6.15 electric bill. "That's the end of our broadcasting, Lord," C. W. says. "Are you telling me to pack it in and head back to the states? Did you really send me here, or is it all a mistake? How can we go on?"

. . . *April 1950.* Jones is walking along the dark Hudson River, crying out to God. "Where did I go wrong? Dick has gone. Left home without a word. Dear God, what did I do to drive away my only son?"

. . . *January 1953.* Katherine is in a deep coma following a head-on collision. C. W., head swathed in bandages, wires protruding from his jaw, is wheeled from the operating room of a California hospital. "By God's grace and my skill I have given you a chin," the surgeon says. "But you'll never be able to talk or blow a horn again. If Katherine regains consciousness, she'll have to have both feet amputated. And because of the severe concussion, her mind will never be right. You'll have to place her in a mental institution."

. . . *Thanksgiving Day, 1975.* From his bed in the hospital emergency ward, C. W. can hear the doctor talking to Katherine: "He's going to make it, but we don't know how much damage has been done by the cerebral thrombosis. Cancel all his engagements. He's finished."

But "call unto me," God had said to Clarence Wesley Jones, "and I will show you great and mighty things." Great and mighty things had filled the head and heart of this high school dropout with a dream. . .

. . . a dream that would take him from a poor basement apartment in downtown Chicago and send him trudging through South American jungles and over mountains, driving tractors at dawn and winding transformers at midnight, to stand in wretched Indian huts and presidential palaces.

. . . a dream for missionary radio that was conceived on the windy rooftop of Chicago's City Hall as Clarence blew his trombone into the crude microphone, and as Paul Rader preached in what may have been the first gospel broadcast.

. . . a dream that has grown from a fragile wire strung between two poles sending a whisper of God's love across the city of Quito, swelling now into a mighty shout echoing around the globe. The message is beaming not only from the spectacular towers and antennas of Radio HCJB, the Voice of the Andes, situated on the rooftop of the world, but as well, from the 70 other missionary radio stations that have since come into being, largely because of the inspiration of what God has been able to do through this one man.

Beyond the clouds. Much travel with sound trucks was through and over the majestic Andes Mountains.

Father-strength
is family-strength,
and family-strength
is the foundation
of a strong church,
community,
and nation.
C. W. Jones

There was little hint of the missionary statesman in the boy growing up on Chicago's South Side. If there was, the family did not see him as a special child—just one who needed a lot of spankings.

C. W.'s parents were both deeply involved in the Salvation Army. They had met at a street corner meeting, a Salvation Army function: Emma Detbrener had seen the young officer, George Jones, on his knees leading the invitation hymn. Love had grown between them in the Officers Training School where Emma had soon enrolled. But the Salvation Army regimen was a strict one, and following graduation the young couple was separated for a year. Emma was sent east on tour as a vocalist, and George headed west with his E-flat cornet.

At last they were allowed to marry, and together they served as Salvation Army officers in Duluth, Minnesota. It was a hard life, with their only income what they could pick up at street corner meetings or from the sale of a magazine called *The War Cry*. When the babies came, Emma would snuggle them in a washtub behind the stove and leave them there alone while she went the rounds of the saloons selling the magazines.

The Joneses' first two children died; and when Emma became pregnant again, George decided they would have to have a regular income. At Sherrard, Illinois, he found work as a coal miner, but on Sunday he still captained the little Salvationist work at nearby Rock Island, Iowa, on the Mississippi River.

Clarence Wesley Jones was born on December 15, 1900. Soon after, George and Emma moved into Chicago where George served as janitor of a three-story red brick apartment building; he stepped down from his commissioned rank to become Sergeant Major in the No. 1 Citadel Corps on West Madison Street.

When Clarence started school, it bothered him that his father was a janitor and that they lived in a basement apartment. As soon as he was around the corner, he'd rip off the newspaper leggings his mother had wrapped around his legs to keep out the bitter chill of Chicago winters. Yet they always ate well, and their home was attractive, with "floors so clean you could eat off them," Clarence recalls. Emma would pick up things at the second-hand shop, even her clothes, and by taking a tuck in here or adding a pleat there, managed always to appear as if she had come "straight from Fifth Avenue."

Clarence remembers how trim she looked in her army uniform, her bonnet perched just right, as she played the guitar and tambourine on the street corner Sunday afternoons. He remembers the sharp crease in George's uniform and the shoes always polished on this quiet, solid man who at seventeen had chosen to leave home rather than renounce his allegiance to the Salvation Army. It had been unthinkable that a well-to-do mine manager, a dignified pillar in the Church of England, would have a son making a spectacle of himself parading down the road and preaching on street corners where the Salvation Army workers were often pelted with rocks and rotten eggs. And so the family had disowned young George.

Not long afterwards, George's father had had his back broken in a mine cave-in and had died. Clarence recalls seeing his Grandmother Jones only two or three times; she was an aristocratic lady with elegant hat and gloves, looking most uncomfortable and out-of-place in their little basement apartment.

Clarence felt proud when his mother told him of the day in

Duluth when the saloon owner came dashing down the street with his team of horses, determined to crash right into the marching Salvation Army lads and lassies, and thus break up their parade. But Captain George Jones grabbed the reins of the horses and held them back, and this so infuriated the man that with his whip he lashed George repeatedly across the back, cutting through his uniform until the blood flowed. Courageously, George held firm until his group had passed to safety.

Yes, although only five feet nine inches and 145 pounds, George Jones was very strong. Indeed, Clarence knew how strong his father's arms were whenever his father led him into the bathroom and took the razor strap off the door for a spanking. But Emma was always close by, and before long she would quietly say, "That's enough, George," and the strokes would stop. Later she would let young Clarence brush her long hair, and this somehow comforted him.

Clarence felt close to his mother, who seemed to have a warm, healing touch. One day, Clarence chased a ball out into the road, tripped, and fell right under a team of prancing delivery horses. They pulled him out, badly hurt, and carried him to his mother who miraculously nursed him back to health. ("We didn't rush off to hospitals in those days.") Another time, when Clarence's tonsils were to come out, they made the ascent to an upper floor apartment, probably to have more light on the kitchen table, and mother again was the nurse.

There were times when Clarence would become very angry with his father. Clarence remembers vividly how his father would argue with the streetcar conductor each Sunday whether or not Clarence, tall for his age, should pay adult fare. "I'd become embarrassed, then very angry, especially because father was in full Salvation Army uniform. Father would say it was the principle of the thing."

Clarence's young life was brightened when he met his eighth-grade teacher. "She was lovely, handsome, kind, compassionate, and I fell in love with her. But I also fell in love with my Sunday School teacher; and when I learned she was going to be married, I was devastated. I used to walk up to where she lived and cry and cry."

The highlight of each year came when Clarence, mother Emma, and little brother Howard, who had arrived on the scene seven years after Clarence, set off for Milwaukee, a trip of some ten hours, traveling on what they called the "Whaleback," a rounded novelty of a ship with cabins perching precariously on top as she wallowed and rolled up Lake Michigan.

There they were greeted by the erect old Prussian soldier and his short, plump wife—Grandfather John and Grandmother Bertha Detbrener. Then they'd be launched into exquisite summers of playing on log rafts and fishing for bullheads in Lake Winnebago, which was just across the road from the Detbrener's home. Mornings they would gorge themselves on sweet German coffeecake topped with fresh peaches, and later in the day they'd sneak a dill pickle from the big barrel at the bottom of the basement stairs.

Grandfather Detbrener worked for the Sault Ste. Marie Line of the railway. He'd lost a leg, so they'd made him a flagman at a level crossing. When a train was approaching, he'd hobble from his little sentry box to hold up a warning sign. Each noon, Clarence had the job of picking up a five-cent pail of "suds" from the local tavern and taking it to his good German grandfather. "Who'd ever want to touch this smelly stuff?" young Clare wondered.

After work, the old soldier would pull out scrapbooks with pictures and clippings and fight the wars all over again for the two enthralled youngsters. Later in the evening, when he had hauled himself out onto the porch where he liked to sit and rock, watching the sun going down over the lake, Howard and Clarence would sneak under the porch and start a hissing, yapping cat-and-dog fight that would get the old grandfather whacking on the boards with his cane.

Clarence got the idea he would like to make some toy soldiers. One day he sneaked up to his grandfather's room where he pulled out the precious scrapbooks from under the bed. Clarence was studying the war pictures intently when he heard Grandfather coming up the stairs, dragging his wooden leg. "Vere is Clarence?" his grandfather called. Clarence was terrified. Hastily he shoved the books back under the bed and scurried out the window, where he hung from the sill until Grandfather had gone elsewhere to look.

That summer, Clarence made a whole army out of poured lead, complete with tents and cannons, infantry, and cavalry— hundreds of pieces—"for his brother's Christmas present." Whether Howard wanted toy soldiers was something Clarence didn't bother to ask.

Clarence was always making something with his hands, and when company came, he'd occasionally disappear under his bed so he could keep on working. His tolerant mother smiled and let him carry on. One year the boys chiseled a magnificent thirty-inch boat out of a railway tie; but when they hauled this wondrous creation to the dock for launching, it sank like deadweight to the bottom.

Sometimes they'd visit Uncle Andy and Aunt Helen in Waukesha, Wisconsin. Clarence liked it best when he and Howard went by themselves because the more liberal Vohs household gave him a chance to get away from the religiously close, restricting influence of his parents. The Vohses owned an elite butcher shop and each day sent Clarence to deliver meat to the many resort hotels. The team of horses knew the way so well that often while Clare was in the hotel, they'd start out, leaving Clarence to run and catch up.

The Vohses knew Clarence was frightened of the dark. At night they'd all be sitting on the front porch when Uncle Andy would say, "It's time to go to bed, Clarence." Young Clarence remembers one night starting up the dark stairs, trembling, when suddenly a sheet came tumbling down around him. Uncle Andy roared at the joke, but Clarence never forget the terror of it. When Clarence later turned into a practical joker, that memory probably kept him from playing the same kind of prank.

The Detbreners were devout Methodists, but Grandmother was enthusiastic for any kind of church service. One evening she took Clarence with her to what he could only describe as a "holy roller meeting," and the episode turned the young Jones against any sort of religious demonstration just about as much as the smell of the saloon turned him away from drinking.

During his school years, Clarence was a good athlete and a competitive one, earning perhaps more than his share of scrapes and batterings in baseball and hockey games from which he still carries the scars. A bout with "TB of the glands" laid him up for six months.

Clarence was fortunate to have teachers who encouraged his creativity in writing and art of all sorts: wood carving, metal work, painting. Some of his pieces are still treasured by relatives. However, after two years of high school, feeling bored and unchallenged by what to him were mostly meaningless subjects, the fifteen-year-old Jones persuaded his parents to let him drop out, and he got a job at Montgomery Ward wrapping and shipping tires. The war was on, and every time young Clarence stepped off the elevated railway on his way to or from work, some brash young girls would accost him: "Where is your service button?" Embarrassed and fed up with the daily badgering, Clarence went to a volunteer booth and lied about his age so they would give him a service button.

After working at Montgomery Ward, he was employed as a draftsman in an engineering firm. By now, Clarence's father had gotten a job with Western Electric and they had moved to a second floor duplex. Compared to what they had been living in, the new home seemed beautiful—even luxurious. "How marvelous," Clarence says, remembering that time. "I was so proud!"

Clarence was playing regularly now in the Salvation Army Band where his father was Sergeant Major. For years Clare had been asking when he could join. Finally, George Jones took the twelve-year-old to band practice, and Clarence started learning the E-flat alto horn. "I guess I was a natural, and just played by instinct," Clarence figures. He took a turn on the baritone horn, and then the euphonium. Then one night the trombonist didn't show up for practice. "Can I take his part?" young Clarence inquired. So he went along on the march, finding the seven positions on the slide trombone as he went, and by the time the band had returned to the citadel, Clarence Jones was hooked. This was his instrument.

His whole world began to revolve around music. "It wasn't so much that I wanted to achieve for myself; I wanted to play well for the sake of the band, to help them win honors." During those years in the Salvation Army, Clarence Jones mastered every instrument in the band except the tuba.

I thought I was a Christian.
But now I know
I was just as big a sinner
as those bums
we've been preaching to
on West Madison Street.
C. W. Jones
October 1918

There was only one problem in playing with the Salvation
Army Band: when they'd be on the street corner, the leader,
often Clarence's father, would frequently call for testimonies. If
none was forthcoming, he'd begin to single out different members. Or worse: "We'll go around the circle," he'd say. At this
point Clarence had no testimony. He had no personal experience with nor commitment to Jesus Christ. So when his turn
drew ominously near, try as he might, he could not manu-
facture a testimony. Time after time, to his secret humiliation,
he could only smirk and mutter a "Ditto" or "The same goes
for me" to the last chap's witness.

One of their neighbors was Richard Oliver, Sr., who used to
play in the Salvation Army Band with the Joneses, but now
directed the music at the new Moody Tabernacle. One day,
Oliver stopped by and asked George Jones if he and Clarence
would play in the Moody band. Clarence decided to give it a try,
and he reveled in the varied repertoire, which included not only
hymns but favorite band numbers such as "Stars and Stripes
Forever" and other stirring Sousa marches. Between Paul Rader's
preaching and the musical attractions, they were packing the
5000 seats at the Tabernacle.

Richard Oliver, Jr., was an accomplished pianist, and he and

Clarence, just eight days apart in age, hit it off from the start. They soon were dubbed "David and Jonathan." Oliver, Sr., quickly recognized Clarence's unusual musical ability, and offered to tutor him, even though Clarence refused to get up at 4 A.M. to practice as Richard, Jr., did. Clarence and Richard began to swap expertise, with Jones teaching Richard how to play tennis and baseball, the sports he'd never had time for, and Richard teaching Jones piano, and persuading Clarence to go to the American Conservatory for studies in harmony and composition.

Clarence sat through five Sundays at Moody Church wrapped up in the music, immune to anything else. "But on the sixth Sunday, October 27, 1918, Paul Rader was speaking directly to me," Clarence recollects. "I don't know what his sermon was, but when Rader gave the invitation, I knew I had to respond. Then I looked at those 5000 people, and wondered what they would think when I got up out of the band and went to the altar. But I had to go. As I passed Rich at the grand piano, his face was beaming with joy because he'd been praying for me."

Back in the inquiry room, Clarence figured he knew the routine: after all, he'd seen sinners by the dozens at the Salvation Army penitent form. So he dropped to his knees, bowed his head, mouthed a prayer, and within thirty seconds was on his way out the door again. "Fortunately a big burly chap intercepted me," Jones recalls.

"Where are you going?" he asked.

"I'm saved now, so I'm leaving," Clarence replied.

"How do you know you're saved?"

"Why, I feel better," Clarence answered.

That was hardly enough. "Suppose you have a toothache tomorrow. How are you going to feel then? If you are going to last, my boy, you need to put your feet on the solid rock of God's Word." Then that wise man led him through Scripture verses till at last Jones could say, "I know I'm saved because God's Word says so."

That week Jones reported to the Salvation Army bandmaster that he was leaving because he'd been saved. "What do you mean? You have always been saved. You've been coming to the Army all your life. Your father is the Sergeant Major."

Jones could only reply: "I thought I was a Christian. But now I know I was just as big a sinner as those bums we've been preaching to on West Madison Street." This experience made a deep impression on Clarence Jones, that all those years he could be making a public profession as a child of God without having the grace of God in his heart and life.

Very soon, the whole family had moved to Moody, "blessed by Rader's ministry about the Second Coming of Christ, and enjoying the Lord's Table. All this was new to these Army folk," Jones relates.

Just two weeks after his conversion, Clarence had gone over to the Sunday afternoon Christian Companionship Club at Moody. (The Tabernacle did not open until three o'clock for Bible School.) A missionary from Japan presented a tremendous message, and then he asked if there were any who would give themselves to God for service. Right away Clarence's hand shot up. He was sure that every one of the 100 young people would answer the call. But as he stood to his feet, to his surprise, he was the only one. "What is the matter with these people?" he thought. "The Lord has done so much for them!" No matter. "I've got Christ as my Savior. I'll be glad to do anything he wants, go any place he sends me," this young believer responded.

That very week, he was knocking on the door at Moody Bible Institute. "What course do you want to take?" they asked. "Why, the missionary course." What else indeed? He didn't know that this was an answer to Emma and George Jones's prayers until his mother began to cry for joy when Clarence told them his plans.

The three years at Moody skipped by with Clarence indeed studying practical "missionary" subjects and also theology. Down in the basement they had fixed up a shop where students were required to fashion various equipment and cooking utensils out of scraps of tin and wood. Clarence proudly remembers the coffee pot he made, and pies whipped up in home economics.

Three pals from the church had joined him: Richard Oliver, Jr., Lance Latham, and Howard Ferrin. The four made up a fun-loving if not formidable tennis team.

The day after graduation in 1921, as class president with top honors, Clarence left Chicago to go on tour with evangelist Charles Neighbour, down through the coal-mining state of West Virginia.

Love is
a fragile flower
needing cultivation
if it is to grow
C.W. Jones

Returning from West Virginia, Neighbour and his young song leader came to the little town of Lima, Ohio, where the godly Rev. Adam Welty ran a rescue mission for the hoboes and bums. As Clarence shook hands with Welty, he saw coming down the stairs Welty's stunningly beautiful sixteen-year-old daughter Katherine. "This is it!" something in his heart said.

During the special meetings, Clarence led the children's and young people's services, and Katherine played the piano; and so they had to practice together. "Clarence was very handsome, and such a talented song leader and trombonist," Katherine recalls. And Clarence saw a beautiful Christian girl who loved the Lord and was greatly loved by her dignified father. Before the two-week campaign was over, Clarence was admittedly in love.

"She's much too young to consider marriage," Welty said when Clarence very properly asked for her hand in marriage. "She has to finish high school and go to college yet. And probably Bible school."

Back in Chicago, where Clarence had joined forces with Paul Rader in a new ministry, the young Jones kept up the courtship, writing letters and beautifully illustrated love poems, and sending a box of chocolates every week. (Never maraschino cherries, because that was what her other suitor brought her. Although only sixteen, Kath had virtually been engaged when Clarence appeared on the scene.)

When word leaked out at the Tabernacle that Clarence had fallen for a high school girl, there was chagrin. "With 5000 girls here, why did you go off to Ohio and choose someone from the cradle?" they wanted to know. Nevertheless, at every chance Jones would break away from his work for a quick visit to Lima.

Not all of Katherine's family was excited about this romance. Clarence hadn't been to college. This did not sit too well in a family where one uncle was a United States senator and a brother was a graduate of Princeton and studying law. But these Swiss Weltys were a musical family: Fred was a tenor soloist with the famous Westminster Choir, brother Roy, the Princeton grad, could yodel beautifully, while Katherine's father played the piano "with the music upside down." Gradually, the Weltys began to respect the professional musicianship of the young Jones. Also, Clarence had a delightfully quick wit and the ability to fit easily into any situation.

In high school Katherine's grades were outstanding. She had superb secretarial skills and had won a typing contest for the western half of the state. In college she was offered a scholarship in literature and creative writing at Harvard. But Katherine had by now also been captivated by love (though she was not yet admitting it to Clarence).

Katherine spent one summer at Nyack Bible Training College. Later, her year as a young school teacher flew by, with Clarence popping up beside her to carry home her books or to escort her to a box social where he had to bid an astronomical $1.00 for his nineteen-year-old sweetheart's lunch, containing his favorite whipped cream tarts.

Katherine's mother had died when Kath was only three years old. Adam Welty later married again, and although his new wife did a fine job of keeping the family together and looking after Rev. Welty, the burden of raising Kath seemed to have rested with Adam. Consequently, Rev. Welty, doting on his little *schatzelie*, was somewhat overprotective and therefore strict that the young couple should not be left alone. Once, when he did let them out alone, it was in a rainstorm, and Clarence and Katherine spent a rapturous day walking about Lima, Ohio, under an umbrella.

One summer the Weltys attended a conference near Cleveland where Clarence was leading the singing. After the service, the young Jones managed to take Katherine out for a late drive. As he leaned over in the front seat to kiss her, Katherine called out, "You're going to hit the bridge!" Clarence, startled, swerved back onto the road.

That was the night Katherine finally said yes to Clare. He'd proposed every time he was with her, and Kath was afraid he wouldn't ask her again.

And what happened to that interrupted kiss? "Clarence never started anything he didn't finish," is all Katherine will say.

They were married when Kath was almost twenty and Clare was going on twenty-four. The wedding took place in the living room above the rescue mission, with Lance Latham at the piano and Richard Oliver, Jr., as best man. Paul Rader had come in by train that morning, and the ceremony moved along smoothly until the ringbearer dropped the ring. Rader began to pray—and he prayed all around the world—while Richard got down on his knees and searched the carpet. Finally, the ring was discovered under Clarence's left shoe. Rader, who had been watching the whole charade apprehensively, concluded the prayer with a mighty, "Hallelujah!" and proceeded through the vows.

At the reception, Paul Rader handed Clarence a roll of bills: "Go to Baltimore next week and set up tent meetings for us. That will be your honeymoon." So they set off in a borrowed Ford, and in downtown Baltimore found an excellent vacant lot for Rader's big 150 x 60 foot tent, complete with sawdust trail.

Going on to Philadelphia, they encountered opposition and found all church doors closed to Paul Rader's ministry. So with fall coming on, Clarence rented a local arena, and they packed it out night after night with Rader's powerful preaching and Clarence's lively song leading and trombone playing. The crowds loved the new gospel songs which were just then coming into vogue, such as the favorite "Glory Song" and "When We All Get to Heaven." Jones was already composing some hauntingly beautiful numbers himself, and these thrilled the audiences.

In Atlantic City the meetings were again successful. One night the hotel manager prepared a special dinner party for the team, but Katherine and Clarence unassumingly thought that it was only for Rader, and they spent the night walking the boardwalk, eating hot dogs, never realizing that the banquet had been prepared for them as well. Finally Lance Latham caught up with them: "We're all waiting for you!" he said. Somehow, the young couple managed to eat a "grand dinner" on top of all those hot dogs.

Returning to the Chicago Gospel Tabernacle, the same girls who had swarmed around Clarence and the other attractive eligible men, now welcomed Clarence's bride. "Who could help but love Katherine?" they said, and soon Kath was very much part of the team.

At last,
we're going
to fight Satan
in his own territory—
the air!
Paul Rader

Clarence's call back to Chicago had come after approximately a year on the road with Charles Neighbour. One day in 1922 he'd received a telegram from his old music master, Richard Oliver, Sr.: "Paul Rader starting new Tabernacle. Will you come and play in brass quartet?" Jones jumped at this "call from God," as he took it to be, and the chance to minister with this giant of a man who was his spiritual father, and through whose mighty ministry and missionary vision Clarence had been stretched and challenged during his Moody years. As Clarence expresses it: "I suppose more than any other man, Paul Rader influenced me for God and the gospel, putting things into my life that have formed the warp and woof fabric for Christian service later. I have always thanked God for the impression in my life as a young Christian that came through the tremendous ministry of Paul Rader, with his common-sense approach, his balanced judgment, his great love of the Word of God, and his tremendous emphasis on the message of grace."

Vibrant and dynamic, Rader was a man of tremendous charisma, one of the great evangelistic preachers; his personal discovery of the Second Coming of Christ charged his messages with a compelling intensity and immediacy that drew huge crowds night after night. And more: God had burdened him with a vision of a world dying without Christ, a vision that lifted his eyes beyond the four walls of Moody Church to make the whole world his parish. "I have seen the vision and for self I cannot live; life is worse than useless till my all I give," he had written.

To that vision God had added a determination and faith, communicated not only in his powerful preaching, but in hymns like Rader's "Only believe—all things are possible, only believe." There was an obvious anointing on his life and ministry.

In 1922 Rader had left Moody, and what he felt was a limited ministry, and was involved in international evangelism when a group of supporters prevailed upon him to return to Chicago where they would build a great evangelistic center for the whole city of Chicago, and a base for his beloved missionary outreach, "The Worldwide Christian Couriers." Located where Barry, Halsted and Clark Streets come together on Chicago's North Side, the Chicago Gospel Tabernacle was little more than a huge rough barn, "a wretched-looking place," as Kathryn Titcomb, Rader's younger sister, described the unpainted board walls, the sawdust, and later the crushed-rock floor and hard wooden benches with straight slat backs. Three great stoves down each aisle threw a good heat.

But it was a friendly place, and everyone felt welcome. Kathryn Titcomb recalled one evening when just for fun she asked the streetcar conductor, "Is this where Paul Rader preaches?" The conductor replied, "Yeah, a lot of crazy people go there. You can go along with them."

Crazy or not, 5000 people packed the Tabernacle every night of the week as Rader preached for an amazingly quick hour with a fervor that so drenched him in sweat that he had to shower and change after every service.

Rader was one of the first of the evangelists to recognize the powerful influence music could be in a service, and he used it both to attract a crowd and to set the mood for his message. Consequently the appalling conditions of the Tabernacle were easily overridden, not only by the good preaching but by the wonderful music. Mrs. Titcomb recalls with enthusiasm, "It was so entertaining we wouldn't miss it for anything. We were there every night in the week; otherwise we thought we were back-slidden!"

For a half-hour before each service, Rich Oliver and Lance Latham gave a thrilling concert on the twin Mason-Hamlin grand pianos; then the choir would sing several of the spirited new gospel songs, the band would play rousing arrangements, the brass quartet would perform, and the popular Jones brothers would do a duet. Howard, seven years younger, was still in short pants when he began to blend his cornet with Clarence's trombone, and in those nine years at the Tab, the duo developed a "golden tone," a sweetness and brilliant virtuosity that won them an acclaim not excelled in the gospel music of that day, and perhaps not since. Their playing of "Christ Arose" at an Easter Sunrise Service in Soldiers Field where they were the major attraction became an unforgettable experience for thousands attending. "Together they made beautiful music. They were dedicated to their music and to their Lord."

Carlton Booth commented that he "never knew anyone who could play a message on the trombone with such dexterity and skill as Clarence Jones." Listening to early recordings, an artist with the CBC (Canadian) Network commented that Clarence Jones's musicianship was such that had he chosen the secular world, undoubtedly he would have gone to the top. Co-workers remember studio sessions when Clarence, although totally professional in his demand for excellence, with his beautiful sense of humor and spontaneity was always equal to any emergency—a joy to work with, and with none of the prima donna temperament.

During those years at the Chicago Gospel Tabernacle, Rader managed to gather around him an unusually gifted group of brilliant young musicians, mostly conservatory trained, some of whom had performed with the Chicago Symphony. The inspired young composer and pianist, Merrill Dunlop, had joined the team, as had an exceptional trumpeter, Jimmy Neilson.

Quickly Rader discovered that these young people were equal to anything he threw at them. Almost all were "cracker-jack musicians" who not only could play an instrument well, but could arrange and direct various ensembles.

When Mayor William Hale Thompson called and said, "We need some musicians to help with programs on our new radio station," it was small wonder that Rader jumped at the chance. "Sure, we'll come," he told the mayor. To his staff, he said: "We'll take our gospel songs right into the homes, the hotels and saloons, even the bawdy houses—every place where there is a receiver. At last, we're going to fight Satan in his own territory—the air!" Rader was elated.

On a windy afternoon, June 17, 1922, Rader and his brass quartet climbed to the roof of the old City Hall in downtown Chicago. Richard Oliver, Sr., and Clarence were on trombone, Howard Jones and Oral Thomas were on trumpet, standing in front of Chicago's first Radio Station, WHT, in honor of the mayor. What they saw was a small booth constructed of rough pine boards with no roof on it, and a small hole cut out in one side. "Point your instruments at that hole, and when we say play, you play," they were ordered.

A hand pushed an old telephone through the hole. "Play!" "And we blew our heads off for several numbers, then Rader preached. We were scarcely able to hear ourselves above the noise of the wind and traffic below."

But all across the city of Chicago, on those first little crystal sets, they were heard. "Radio grew by leaps and bounds, and so did our vision," Jones remembers of those early days of radio. "It wasn't long before we were working our heads off, having the greatest time in the world, getting the gospel out to people." With Clarence as program director, soon the Gospel Tab was broadcasting fourteen hours each Sunday over five local stations, and from 7 A.M. to 8 A.M. daily on the CBS network. The mail poured in—thousands of letters weekly.

"Clarence was always coming up with new gospel songs, new ideas," and Latham remembers especially his flair for interesting program introductions.

The daily "Breakfast Brigade" supplied listeners with a regular supply of spiritual food in a "knapsack," which was actually nothing more than a glorified envelope, designed by Jones and containing excerpts of Rader's messages, poems, and music. For the Sunday afternoon program when people could phone in and request special selections to be "dedicated" to their friends—impromptu piano duets, brass quartets, solos, whatever—they needed twenty-five telephone operators to handle the calls.

After the Sunday evening service, Rader pulled out all the stops for the "March of the Ages" radio program, with Clarence directing a choral group and a brass quartet. " 'Tonight I'm going to preach on the "Walls of Jericho," ' Rader would say to us right on the platform just before the message. The auditorium would be darkened, with spotlights on the stage. It was all very dramatic," Jones recalls.

"And then in his sermon Rader would pause and point to us musicians, and we were expected to produce the appropriate sound effects on the spot—marching around the walls, or a trumpet fanfare. And we'd do it, using solos, duets—everybody would be on the edge of their seats—and somehow we'd pick up the cue and improvise. I personally would play a variety of instruments. One night I drew a violin bow across an ordinary saw for the rustling of the wind in the mulberry trees.

"The story of Namaan made a memorable sermon; he'd go down, down into the water and the music would go down. And then he'd come up. When he came up for the seventh time, clean, we had a veritable Hallelujah Chorus!"

At other times, Rader would give the music staff his sermon topic a few days ahead. "Somebody make up a song," he'd ask. And they would, every member of this superb team tossing off beautiful lyrics and melody week after week. Lance Latham, Richard Oliver, Jr., Merrill Dunlop, Jimmy Neilson, Howard Jones, and Clarence, who kept track of the twenty-nine songs he wrote during this time—all used syncopated rhythms and many of the same lush harmonic progressions as the showtunes of the 1920s. (The Tabernacle later published "Gospel Songs of the

Air," a compilation of seventy-six of these selections, including several that Rader wrote.)

Clarence also laid out the orchestrations. "He wrote music as if he were writing a letter," coworkers said. "Most of the music on the Back Home Hour was either written or arranged by C.W."

"We were all in our teens and early twenties, and Rader would trust us kids with hard jobs and fully expect us to do them. And somehow we did," Lance Latham and Clarence both agree. "We'd practice our heads off all week, and by Sunday everything would be ready. We'd hand Paul Rader the typed program, and every once in awhile he'd scrunch it up, toss it in the wastebasket, and just 'wing it,' " Clarence remembers with amazement. "He'd call on us for anything he'd ever heard us do, and we'd do it. We learned that *sometimes the Lord gives you excellence in immediate obedience. You can't know your capacity until you draw on it.*"

There was a tremendous oneness of mind between Rader and the group, so that even when totally unrehearsed (as the most popular 11 P.M. to 12 A.M. Sunday night Back Home Hour usually turned out to be) the listeners thought they had practiced for weeks. "There were no schools of radio to study at, so we made our mistakes and just went on."

Very quickly Clarence emerged as a born pro, an all-round natural in this brand new, untried field. "There have been many good program directors, announcers, engineers, and so on, but no one, either in Christian or secular radio, combines all of these abilities as Clarence Jones has from the start," Lance Latham maintains. "I rate him as the greatest man radio has ever known, unequivocally." (An engineer in Quito later described Jones's announcer's voice as "wonderful, with very low distortion. On the scope, his voice was like little round potatoes running down a ramp.")

In those pioneer days of Christian radio, there were the conservatives who could not see "using the devil's tool" for mass evangelism, so some were preaching against radio even while God was blessing the Tabernacle programs. However,

Paul Rader was not one to take too much notice of opposition, and rather preferred to go ahead with the job the Lord had given him to do, and he instilled this same spirit in his staff. The call letters of the new Chicago Station WJBT became a Tabernacle slogan: "Where Jesus Blesses Thousands."

"I have always been happy for the privilege of training under a man with a positive approach to the gospel message," Clarence Jones affirms.

Infighting
among personnel
is more devilish,
desperate,
and devastating
than anything
from the outside.
C. W. Jones

Almost from the time when Oliver, Sr., had invited Clarence to join in the music ministry of the new Tabernacle, a conflict had been building between the two: Oliver, Sr., the father of Clare's best friend, the bandmaster and choirmaster at the Tab, and Clarence's former teacher; Clarence, winning the plaudits of the crowds with his beautiful music, and now with his unusual ability, becoming Rader's brilliant right-hand man in the glamorous new field of radio. "It's not always easy for a teacher to watch a pupil catch up to him and then spurt ahead," one colleague suggested. "These young people were having opportunities that the older men, like Oliver, Sr., and Jones, Sr., never had."

For whatever reasons, as Clarence played tombone in the band, and on every possible occasion, Oliver, Sr., continually singled him out with unreasonable demands, to the point of being tyrannical. "Seven days of each week we were supposed to be working together," Jones recalls, "out on the platform and before the microphones, leading in happy, joyful praise to God. And all the while it was like a steel saw grating against raw nerves."

For four years Clarence waited before the Lord, through the pioneering of radio, through his early years of marriage, looking for a way to resolve this deteriorating relationship. Often he'd come home and say to Katherine, "I don't know how much more of this abuse and public humiliation I can take. Should I just walk away from it? Leave the Tab?" That was unthinkable. Somehow Clarence kept the turmoil from showing. "His enthusiasm for the Lord always shone forth in his life," many people said.

Finally Clarence went to Rader: "Mr. Oliver has been giving me a very bad time. Something is going to happen between us soon, and I don't want this."

"I've known all along, my boy," Rader admitted. "I've let you go through this discipline to test you, to see how you would react under such pressure and conflict. Now we'll make it up to you." (Jones feels it would have helped him immeasurably through those very difficult years to have known that Rader was aware of the situation and that he was only waiting for the right time to lift Clarence out of it.)

From that point on, Jones was ordained and put in places of decision making and administration. He was appointed song leader and eventually took charge of the whole music department; he was made totally responsible for planning the radio ministry; as well, he had the task of lining up speakers for Rader's absences, and also of "giving some of them the gate when they didn't work out!"

"In fact, everything that came along was pushed C. W.'s way. And no matter what we gave him to do, he always produced," Rader's sister, Kathryn Titcomb, remarked. "And he did it without any fuss. Although Clarence blew a horn, it was never for himself."

Jones was given the job of regularly decorating the Tabernacle. Especially when they brought in missionaries from around the world for the annual missionary convention, the young fellows and girls on the radio staff would all be climbing up stepladders and inching along the steel girders, stringing lights and crepe paper streamers, and draping flags. At Christmas they'd dangle giant stars from the roof and paint a nativity scene across the whole back of the platform. For times when the crowds might

not fill the 5000 seats, rather than have empty spaces, Clarence
rigged up a great tent right inside the tabernacle, with canvas
walls that could be drawn in or pushed back as required. "In-
tents evangelism," they called it.

"We never thought of the hours, or that we might be putting
in 'overtime,'" Jones recalls. More than once an evangelist said
to them: "Come with me and I'll give you four times what
you're making here and you won't have to work so hard."

"But we wouldn't think of it," says Jones. "God had called us
to the Tab and that was our training ground. He was putting
some stamina—a spiritual backbone—into us, teaching us how
to live victoriously under the ministry of Paul Rader.

"And we were having a grand time getting something done
and winning souls. The Tabernacle was growing by leaps and
bounds; thousands of people came and hundreds were saved.
So we just laughed at these offers and went right back to our
grind again, happy as could be."

Paul Rader never asked these young people whether they had
done a task before; he'd just say, "Here's a job we need to do for
the Lord and here's what I'd like to have done, and this is the
way to do it." Clarence recalls: "He would hand us the job and
expect us to produce results. With that kind of challenge, he
drew the very best out of us, and in sheer loyalty to the Lord and
to him, we worked our heads off."

Consequently, when Clarence was asked to organize boys'
and girls' work, something with which he'd had no experience
except for teaching Sunday School, he had to start from scratch.
Clarence brought in Rich Oliver, Lance Latham, and Virginia
Highfield (Lance and Virginia were later married), and they
came up with a simple formula for organizing the "Tabernacle
Scouts" along the lines of the "Boy Scouts," but incorporating
more of the Word of God into the program.

Soon scores of boys eight years old to mid-teens were meeting every Saturday afternoon at the Tab. When summer came,
they boarded the boat for a rough trip across Lake Michigan,
then lugged everything over the fields to Berrien Springs Camp-

ground where they set up a few tents and "had a wonderful two weeks with the boys."

The Tabernacle Scouts led directly into the AWANA Youth Association with some 8000 boys and girls clubs now meeting in twenty-eight countries around the world. Clarence is regarded as the originator of the AWANA program, and Lance Latham is still president of AWANA International.

Paul Rader started a Christian day school where they all took turns teaching. As well, there was a short stint tucked into these busy years when Rader asked Jones to pastor the White City Gospel Tabernacle in an amusement park area on the South Side of Chicago. Clarence's pal from Moody days, Howard Ferrin, had left there to become principal of Dudley Bible Institute in Massachusetts, which later became Barrington College. Paul Rader had an interest as president of the school. For several months, each Sunday the Joneses drove to the South Side for the services, then dashed back across Chicago in time for the 11 P.M. Back Home Hour.

One of the biggest challenges thrown at Clarence was to develop and manage the Maranatha Campground at Muskegon Heights ("Lake Harbor" it was called then), which Rader had bought from the Methodists. There were buildings to be repaired, new ones added, the golf course improved. There were the speakers and musicians to book, and the staff to be hired and directed. Clarence took a special interest in the young staff— counseling them, leading them around the campfire and in raids on the kitchen! They all looked up to Clarence and respected this "intense and dedicated individual, who obviously had a goal in life and lived according to the way the Lord wanted him to live," as Dan Pagenta, a young greenskeeper at the camp summed it up.

It was a hectic schedule the nineteen Tabernacle radio staff kept. Rader went out to many towns for meetings and he would take the brass quartet and some soloists. Often they'd drive all night to be in Chicago for the 7 A.M. Breakfast Brigade (Paul Rader didn't sleep much) or end up at the campground late Sunday night; they'd work there all week, come back to Chicago on Saturday, and start on Sunday again. Sometimes they'd still be preparing and practicing in the car on the way to the studios.

These bright young people obviously created a lot of fun wherever they went. Rader's daughter, Harriet, recalls especially the happy Christmas Eve serenades when the brass quartet would come in from the cold to hot oyster stew in front of a blazing fire.

And then Clarence brought home his lovely bride, and before long they had two little girls, Marian and Marjorie. Harriet Rader sometimes babysat out at the campground where they were next-door neighbors. "The Joneses were such wonderful parents. I can see C. W. yet, going down the path with a baby on his shoulders."

Yet Kath had not been happy to be pregnant, and was especially sick during her first pregnancy, spending almost the whole time in bed, first at Mother Jones's and then with Louise Genn, a widow from the church. "I just couldn't cope with anything," Katherine recalls. "Perhaps it was psychological. I'd had such grand plans to go ahead with my music in Chicago." P. R. (as the staff called Paul Rader) spent a lot of time counseling the rebellious young Katherine, helping her to accept her pregnancies and a miscarriage.

Arise
and go
toward the south. . . .
Acts 8:26

One Sunday morning at Lake Harbor (Maranatha), Paul Rader gave a missionary challenge, and at the invitation, Clarence, who had been leading the singing, went forward to give his life for missionary service. Rader was greatly moved. "God bless him. We need Clarence Jones here in this work. But if God wants him in missionary work, that is what we want for him."

Not long after, C. W. was sitting in the service at Lake Harbor as missionaries Ed and Carol Carlson told of their work in Tibet; but what tugged at Clarence's heart was their personal tragedy in having both children die on the long trek home. Yet tears of joy were on their cheeks as they told of their experiences of walking with God in very difficult situations. Despite their sorrow and loss, they were going right back to the place where God had called them.

"I thought of my two little girls in the cottage with Kath—Marian just turned two, and the new baby. What if it had been them? Would I be willing to give them up?"

The Lord spoke to Clarence Jones that night in a voice so clear that C. W. was sure it had to be audible to all around. Just as God had said to Philip in the book of Acts, "Arise and go south," to Clarence he spoke the same words, but added "with radio."

"Go south with radio? Is that what God has been training me for? What about Kath? Often she has said that one reason she was content to marry me was that she knew with the work I was involved in, I would never be a missionary. And that suited her just fine."

Clarence walked along the beach after the service, his head and heart whirling, yet he felt a strange, quiet certainty. "Here I was in a fervor of missionary zeal, setting up conferences and programs for missions, and now it was turned around, pointing right at me. Would I leave this fruitful work, an area where God obviously was blessing, and set out for a spiritual desert?"

When Clare finally returned to the cottage, he didn't tell Kath of God's call, nor that he had answered yes. But at breakfast the next morning, Clare broached the subject: "Kath, if the Lord were to call us to the mission field, would you be ready to go?" Kath came around the table and wrapped Clare in her arms. "It's all right, dearest heart. Last night while I was putting the babies to bed and you were in the service, the Lord came to me, and very plainly he asked, 'Kath, will you go?' Yes, my love, we will go."

Later that day, Kath and Clare left the little girls with "Moo-Moo," Rader's mother, and walked the path through the sand dunes to the Prayer Tower overlooking Lake Michigan. There they climbed the thirty steps to the first level, then up another eighteen to the privacy of the higher platform where they knelt together. Clarence was twenty-six years old, and Katherine was not quite twenty-three. "We wanted to be absolutely sure that this was not just an emotional 'upsurge,' but was truly a call from the Lord himself. After half an hour, we knew beyond any doubting."

Next came the task of telling Paul Rader that very definitely the Lord was calling them to the mission field. "And this was most difficult," as Clarence recalls. "In 1918, God had made Rader my spiritual father, and together with the eighteen other young fellows on the staff, he'd brought us all along. It was tremendous to have the fellowship and leadership of this man. And now I was proposing to cut myself off from all that."

The next Sunday afternoon, C. W. told Rader of his call. Rader slapped him on the back. "That's wonderful! I have just the place for you in India." (A team of Rader's Worldwide Christian Couriers was already working there.)

"But Mr. Rader, God is not calling me to India. It's to Latin America." Clarence remembers vividly that a cloud passed over Rader's face, and their fellowship was never the same after that. Clarence could only conclude that "we have to get weaned away from men, and thrust into the program of God. Kath and I didn't know where we were going; we just knew that it wasn't where someone else thought we should go. This experience taught us that we have to find God's will for ourselves."

So where were they to go? God was confirming the vision, that it was with radio that Clarence Jones was to minister on "the foreign field." "Go south" was the only direction. Clare and Kath got out the atlas. After studying Latin America and South America, they applied to the Scandinavian Alliance Mission, which is now TEAM, The Evangelical Alliance Mission.

Katherine's sister Ruth and her husband, Chester Churchill, were keenly interested in this development. "It's a harebrained idea," Chet said, "but I'll go along with Clare while he looks the place over." As a contractor, Chet was curious to see if there was work for his company in South America.

Chet and Clare were booked to sail for Venezuela on February 1, 1928, so Clare agreed to come east a few days early and lead the singing at Dudley Bible Institute's Missionary Conference where his good friend Rich Oliver had just come to teach. Clarence stopped in New York to pick up his visa. "But you must have a police affidavit," the Venezuelan Consulate told him. So C. W. went to the Twenty-sixth Precinct. "We can't issue papers for you—you're not a resident of New York City." Finally the District Attorney's office agreed to wire Chicago and get clearance.

Blithely, Clarence hopped on the train for Massachusetts, and that evening did a radio program with Rich and the Dudley Gospel Chorallers. But back at Oliver's a telegram was waiting for Clarence: "Return New York at once." The police report had come back from Chicago: "Clarence Jones wanted on felony charge!"

How to prove it was another Clarence Jones? Clarence ended up in the Criminal Investigation Bureau getting fingerprinted, and there was nothing to do but wait until the fingerprints of the wanted Clarence Jones came over the wire. "Missed the opening Conference service," his diary reports. Jones sweated it out. "Must leave it in the Lord's hands. He is able to work out every detail for his glory. Can do nothing but wait for second wire from Chicago. Find it a test of patience, but he says, 'Be still and know that I am God.'"

Cleared at last, C. W. managed to get up to Dudley for the last day of the Conference, returning late that night to New York where he figured all would be smooth sailing. But Monday morning, again at the Venezuelan Consulate: "We have a new regulation: you need a passport photo." Then at the shipping office: "We cannot issue you a discounted ticket without special letters of authorization." Chet arrived, and they scrambled to get Chet's passport photo and papers, but by then the Venezuelan Consulate was closed.

Tuesday brought more running around, more delays. Finally passports, visas, and tickets were all in order. Chet stopped the taxi on the way to the dock to pick up a Spanish-English dictionary, and just after noon on Wednesday, February 1, their ship pulled away from the pier.

I will
lift up
mine eyes
unto the hills . . . .
Psalms 121:1

Notes from C. W.'s diary:

First day at sea: Get seasick. A little homesick but don't admit it even to myself. There's much business ahead for the King.

Second day: Sea worse—so are we.

For the first few days, Chet and Clare avoided the dining room, picking at the fruit and candy that Kath and Ruth had sent. Each day Clare looked for a quiet place to open his letter from Kath—she'd given him one for every day on the boat.

Most of their fellow passengers were headed for the new oil fields in Venezuela, and on Sunday morning, when Clarence discovered no church had been arranged for, he invited several young men "to read the Word" with him in the salon. Later on the voyage he found someone who could play the piano, so C. W. got out his trombone for a few numbers.

When the ship put into Puerto Rico on the sixth day, Chet and C. W. decided to go ashore. But Clare couldn't seem to get his "land legs" and went staggering down the main street like a drunk, finally falling flat on his face in the gutter. As Chet was helping him to his feet, a policeman arrived on the scene, ready to haul Clarence away. Chet and Clare still aren't sure how they got out of that one or how they managed enough Spanish to convince the policeman that everything was okay.

Back at sea, steaming for Venezuela, Clarence waxed poetic as he walked the deck at midnight. "These moonlight nights are full of romance—only my 'romance' is 1500 miles away." Nevertheless, he penned two poems in his diary that night:

Midnight Meditations 7/02/'28

Restless majesty;
Boundless, fathomless; seething and wind-tossed;
Dashing, slashing, thrashing turbulence;
Laving, lashing; caressing, crushing;
Foaming, frothy, frenzied furiousness.
Mirror of heaven, reflecting the moon beams
Hiding and shielding vast dangers unknown.
Sulking and treacherous, venomous; raging,
Roaring, and tearing with beatings so monstrous;
Merciless night—now so passive—then awful,
Whispering and calling, fair siren alluring,
Beautiful shimmering, buoyance serene.
Triumphs unrivaled, yet slave to man's will;
Dangerous, darksome, deceptive green depths
Blue-silver, gray-white, and dark somber hues,
Clouds, sky-mist shadows with glints all diffused.
Sea waves at midnight—
How like the heart of man! Uncleansed by renewing grace
    and uncalmed by the Lord's peace.

Carried Along 7/02/'28

All I do is rest in this deck chair
or in my little cabin.
No work of mine is required
to move this vessel.
It is carrying me
surely, safely, serenely.
No fretting of mine will help

the propellers go round.
They have an engine for that.

It occurs to me that somehow God runs this universe without my help.
He only asks me to rest,
quiet, get limp
as I used to,
a babe in mother's arms,
As I now slouch in a chair on deck.

What a delight to know
that through life
Jesus will carry me.
Why should I struggle in his arms?

And then C. W. wrote the little chorus which he later set to music:

Carried along by my Saviour,
Carried by strength from above;
Struggling is useless endeavor
When I can be carried by love.

Their first view of Venezuela was "entrancing." "The mountains are covered with the densest foliage," Jones wrote, "extending to the very shorelines where they drop abruptly to the sea. Along a narrow beach a little village nestles. The houses are bright colors—blue, pink, and white—all with red or brown roofs. Fishing boats and scurrying launches dot the blue sea of La Guira harbor, with the colorful Venezuelan flag flying from every vessel."

The following morning, Chet and Clare set out for the capital city. "The road is good concrete," they wrote back to their wives, "winding and turning upon itself a dozen times in a mile, ever climbing higher up the mountainside. We have never seen such scenery before. What a grand vista, looking back over the harbor and out to sea for miles! On and up we go, passing a beauty spot here, a falling cascade there, through the clouds now, and reach Caracas after a delightful hour's drive."

Returning down the mountain that night, Clarence noted that "every so often we passed a little wayside shrine, lighted by a candle so feeble, not only in the little covered shrine but in the hearts of these people. Only the light of God's Word can reveal the glory that makes men hungry for the living Christ."

The seven-week trip was filled with adventure. They visited the oil fields, where they found most of the wells capped because there was no way of transporting it out. "But what a challenging call for evangelism of the most rugged type!"

Climbing up one high mountain, their Model T ran out of gas, so the missionary went to the little huts along the road, prevailing upon the Indians to empty the kerosene out of their lamps. "We put it in the tank, cranked her up, and rode to the top. Then we coasted downhill, for three hours seeing nothing but gray mist through which our headlights could barely penetrate ten feet. Finally, we broke through the clouds into a glorious sunset, and while Swanson drove along the bumpy, crushed-rock road, somehow I scribbled the words and music:

On the Mountain top above the world below,
Where the fruits of vict'ry in abundance grow
There the streams of blessing flow from fountains of His grace,
I've been on the mountain top and seen His face!

I have left the valley lowlands long ago
On my pathway brightly beams a heav'nly glow;
Lifted in His arms to heights I thought could ne'er be mine,
I've been on the mountain top by grace divine.

Another day they set out by horseback—for Clarence "a wild and rugged initiation. The mountain paths are slippery in the rain and the horses find it difficult to find footing."

Whenever Clarence saw a need he pitched in and helped. "Up early, but we whistle while we work on the Swanson home," his diary notes. "Because of high rent they are remodeling so four lady missionaries can live upstairs. Much to do in carpentry and painting. We delayed here a week."

Everywhere Jones went he encouraged the local missionaries who were serving mostly under the Scandinavian Alliance Mission or the Christian and Missionary Alliance. He spoke through interpreters in church services and the schools, sang, and played his trombone. It was the first time the Indians had ever seen or heard such an instrument and they "giggled and laughed with delight." It seemed that some of the missionaries were a "trifle shaky" about using a brass instrument, which they associated with dance bands. Nevertheless, Jones felt it was a "peculiar joy to be able to carol the gospel by this novel means" and it proved to be a drawing card.

Clarence the musician and bandsman was fascinated by the Indian bands. It seemed that every village and hamlet had one, and Clarence, with great verve, described a concert in his diary:

"The band here numbered fifteen men or so, with natty blue uniforms and banged-up, tarnished brass instruments. They stood under one of the arc lights in the plaza, blowing for all they were worth. All music was either by inspiration or from memory, so I couldn't find a reason for the music racks each man had standing before him.

"The leader beat time as mechanically and uselessly as a metronome. No one watched him except at the first note and the last. The first number I heard was a waltz. The bass drum and lonely bass would emphasize the first beat of the measure, and three-quarters of the band would answer on the after-beats. One or two clarinets squeaked melody, and one lone cornetist would twitter in now and then. The drum section was a marvel—both of them. They syncopated and banged away, trying to outdo each other by sheer brawn. They received most of the attention of the crowd—and they deserved it.

"After each piece, which repeated and turned upon itself endlessly, the men would lay down their instruments and scatter to the four winds. I couldn't quite ascertain whether they crawled away in shame or strutted in pride. It was rather dark where I was sitting. When the effects of the preceding number had abated somewhat, the director would step to his rack, give a few raps with his baton and the bandsmen appeared from nowhere.

"Multiply the foregoing from 8:00 to 9:30 P.M., and you have typical band concert in Latin America."

They found the beauty of Venezuela "impossible to describe." But Jones tried. "Today we are driving through grapefruit, banana, and pineapple plantations. Tumbling mountain streams dash by us. It's so wonderfully strange and delightful! With orange blossoms in the ravines and snow-capped peaks before us, it's as if Florida were placed in Colorado! Up and up we go, above the timber line.

"We are in the clouds now, and it's very cold, damp and chilly. They call this point 'The Paramo,' reputed to be the highest traversable auto pass in the world, some 13,660 feet. The sun plays hide-and-seek through the clouds, and when it breaks through, we can see the farm patches with their stone fences far below. On the other side of the valley a farmer is tilling with his oxen. The perch is so steep it seems that at every moment they must fall, for at every step they must brace themselves.

"From the top of a high mountain ravine we suddenly come upon the Blue Wells (Pozos Azules), clear crystal pools of water with a strange blue-tinted reflection from the sky. An exquisite touch by nature! How many times during this trip, as I have viewed one extravagant, colorful scene after another, have the Psalmist's words come to mind: 'When I consider the work of thy hands . . .'

"For half an hour the clouds have hidden all from view but a few feet of the road ahead. It's quite a thrill to realize that just over the edge is a sheer drop of hundreds and sometimes thousands of feet. As we begin our descent, passing out of the clouds, we have an unbroken view for mile upon mile of valleys and gorgeous mountainsides stretching to the very rugged horizon itself, with the silver-banded river streaming down the center of the picture.

"What a Christ, to have created all this and so much we haven't yet seen! Surely 'it hath not entered into the mind of man the things that God hath prepared, even here and now, for those that love Him!' However, a cloud passes over the beauty of the scene when we realize that in scarcely any of the places we can see is there any witness of Life and Him.

"How endless the task of missions seems here in Venezuela at our present slow rate of response! This country is only a small portion of a whole great continent, with many places having no witness for millions. Missionary work could be supplemented and speeded up by the perfectly possible procedure of regular Spanish radio broadcasts. I am more and more impressed with the opportunity for evangelism in all Venezuela, and am spending much time in prayer these days, asking the Lord to do *the great and mighty things.*"

Up in Chicago, little Marjorie was having her first birthday. Kath stood her in the window, looking toward the south. "Your daddy is down there somewhere, and he is thinking of us." The tears were running down Kath's cheeks, and she couldn't stop little Marjorie's crying either.

And where was Clarence? On the mountain top. There in Venezuela, John and Anna Christiansen of the C & MA prepared a special tribute in honor of Marjorie's birthday. Anna baked a chocolate cake, and even managed to get cream from the brewery to churn peppermint ice cream for the party.

The next morning, the missionaries all rose early to say good-bye to this young preacher from America. As they drove around a curve in the road above the town below, Clarence asked to stop. Jones took out his trombone, and just as the sun was rising, the sweet tones of "Holy, Holy, Holy" rang out across the valley. Then the sun burst over the horizon, and the missionaries saw him there on the mountain, silhouetted against the sky, the golden rays of the sun flashing off his gold-plated trombone as he played "God Be With You Till We Meet Again." And then he was gone, up the mountain, and down to the valley, and on to Colombia.

To Colombia, because his approaches to the government in

Venezuela had been fruitless. He'd gone to President Gomez in Caracas asking for a permit to build a noncommercial, non-denominational radio station that would bring news and culture as well as the Word of God to the people. The answer was a flat no.

Jones then went to Colombia. And Panama. And Cuba. The answer was the same. These men did not understand radio, but they knew its power could be a risk. "You would be on the air, filling it with all kinds of things that would turn my people against me," Gomez said.

Clarence came home to Chicago, a confused and frustrated twenty-seven-year-old. "I went to Venezuela so sure they'd come running to me because the Lord had called me there. Instead they ran the other way. 'We have no place for foreigners on the air, or any other place. And we have our religion,' they said."

Clarence felt he had failed. Totally. "So I said to the Lord, 'Where did I get off the beam?' And he reminded me of Paul's being forbidden to speak the word in Asia, and then trying to go to Bithynia—and again the Spirit did not permit them. They passed by Mysia and Troas, and finally the doors opened with the certain call: 'Come over into Macedonia and help us.'"

Still, Clarence felt frustrated and a little embarrassed. He'd spent all that money, taken all that time. And what did he have to show for it? In the back of Katherine's Bible was a quotation: "The wise man of the ages is the man who discovers the direction in which God is moving and moves in that direction . . . ." Maybe he was being headstrong. Maybe the Lord wanted them in India after all. The door was wide open there, and the south was shut tight.

And what of Katherine? Secretly, twenty-three-old Kath was elated! Her initial reckless zeal had worn off, and with two little ones to care for, she just did not want to go to "the foreign field." Not at all.

Not by might,
nor by power,
but by my Spirit.
Zecharaiah 4:6

Clarence was certain of one thing when he came home from South America: he had to have more education. Jones had been impressed with the caliber of the Latin Americans with whom he had had to deal, and realized that if his life's work was to be among them, he'd have to pull up to their level. The YMCA offered morning cram courses, and Clarence jumped into this program, completing two high school years in one. He then enrolled in Northwestern University in suburban Evanston, majoring in zoology, enjoying particularly some good-natured jousting with an evolutionist professor. C. W. was also doing a correspondence course in advertising and public relations, and working three hours each week for an advertising agency, making as much in those three hours as he earned all week at the Tab.

Eighteen months had gone by since the Venezuelan fiasco, with no further light on Clare's vision to "go south with radio." The heavens seemed to be closed to his pleadings for direction. He was still ministering at Chicago Gospel Tabernacle but there were some dark times for Katherine and Clarence: like the day when Clare, accompanied by his dear friend Richard Oliver, rode out to the graveyard in the funeral hearse, tenderly holding a little coffin on his lap, tears falling uncontrollably at the loss of their precious child—who would have been their third—just two days after birth.

Then there was the day of such discouragement that Clarence, desperately needing some money for his family, unable to shake off the feelings of total inadequacy and failure, and chagrined that this obsession with South America had made him look like a fool, decided to chuck it all—his work at the Tabernacle, his call to the mission field, his family—and went down to enlist in the Navy. He was rejected for lack of 20/20 vision.

At this time, the Joneses were living in a rather nice hotel apartment midway between the university and the Chicago Tabernacle. In the fall of 1929, a delightful young couple moved into the same building—Ruth and J. D. Clark. Ruth had taught school with Clarence at the Tab and then had gone to Ecuador where she had married John. Now the Clarks were home on furlough, based in Chicago.

As they sat in the Joneses' apartment drinking hot chocolate with cinnamon toast, night after night Clarence would pump Ruth and John about Ecuador. Kath would be stewing to herself, "Please stop all this talk of South America!"

J. D. was a tall, warmly humorous Britisher from Jamaica who had quickly won the affection of the Ecuadorians, and he spun captivating tales of the incomparable beauty of that exquisite little country, "The Jewel of the Americas," straddling the equator, with towering, snowcapped volcanoes and lush green jungle; of savage headhunters in the Amazon forest, and proud descendants of the Incas shivering in lonely caves or thatched adobe huts on the high Andean slopes. He told of rivers rushing down from the mountains, and the Pacific washing warm against crescent curves of white sand; of enchanting Quito, the oldest capital city in the Americas, once the center of Inca worship and now a treasure store of baroque architecture, set at 9,600 feet, with a climate of year-round May; of food and flowers of every description growing in riotous abundance.

And best of all, Ecuador seemed to have as stable a government as any in South America, and one of the most progressive, with the first hospital and the first university in all of South

America; with beautiful señoritas and gallant señores—a charming, gracious blend of Spanish conquistadores and Inca nobility.

"But wait until the Larsons come," the Clarks would say. "They'll persuade you that Ecuador is the place for your missionary radio."

Consequently, in line with his duties at the Tab, Clarence booked Grace and Reuben Larson to tell of their missionary pioneering among the "savage red men" in the Amazon headwaters of Ecuador.

Now, the Larsons had gone to Ecuador from Wisconsin in 1924 with a vision to reach jungle Indians for Jesus Christ, and were sent to the Quichuas in the Tena area, some seventy-five miles southeast of Quito as the condor flies, but a minimum of eight arduous days of hiking over the mountains, down slippery canyons, and through tangled jungle.

At the junction of two swift rivers, the Tena and the Missauwaali, headwaters of the mighty Amazon, Grace and Reuben had put up a little shelter, hardly more than a grass shack, and tried to make contact with the Indians. As possible trading material, Reuben had brought with him cloth, beads, knives, machetes—all the trappings of a jungle trading post. And he did manage to draw the Indians. They'd sidle into the little store at Dos Ríos ("Two Rivers"), untie grubby red kerchiefs to drop a few coins on the rough counter, take their knife or cloth, and disappear into the forest as silently as they had come.

"But Grace, when am I going to get a chance to talk to these people?" Reuben asked. "I'm sure they're out there watching us from the cover of the forest."

That's exactly what was happening. Every move of Reuben and Grace was being carefully observed, because other, less scrupulous whites, anxious to keep the territory for themselves, were spreading ugly tales of the missionary's baseness and cruelty. The weeks became months as Reuben patiently pushed back the jungle, clearing a little more each day, working on his Spanish and Quichua.

Finally, feeling that their work had been completely fruitless, one Sunday morning Reuben and Grace fell to their knees, absolutely wrenched with a feeling of total failure, crying out in desperation to God for direction. "O God, show us how to break through to these people, or else let us leave."

And as they waited before the Lord, very clearly he gave them the encouragement of Zechariah 4:6: "Not by might, nor by power, but by my spirit."

That verse had been adopted by the Larsons long before they went to the jungle to be the theme of their ministry. "But somehow we'd forgotten it in the busyness of our own efforts. At this point, when finally we had to admit that we were no match for the situation, it warmed our hearts to be reminded so vividly that we weren't in this alone." Reuben recalls that they went about their work for the rest of the day with greatly lightened spirits and renewed confidence, certain that God would intervene and undertake. When and how, they could not know.

The very next morning, Reuben looked up to see two Indian dugout canoes pulling in to shore. "We have come to be your Indians," they said. "We have been watching you, and what they told us about you were all lies. We want to help you clear the jungle and build a better house." They called Reuben "patron," a Spanish term that wraps into one word the roles of father, banker, judge, arbiter, and overseer. Now these Indians slashed away with their machetes, cutting and splitting the bamboo for a proper house, enlarging the clearing, and planting pineapple and coffee trees.

Grace and Reuben, with the help of a few medicines, managed to treat many of the Indians' illnesses. They started a school for the Indians. They improved the mail service, putting an extra courier on the trail to provide weekly delivery. All the while Reuben ministered effectively to these primitives of the upper jungle, not only winning souls with the gospel, but as well, winning a reputation—here was one white man the Indians could trust.

In the midst of this, with telling understatement, the Larsons recorded that they "walked over the ridge [a difficult eight-to ten-day trek] from Dos Ríos to Quito" where Grace shortly delivered a baby girl, Peggy Jo. Three months later, they packed little Peggy Jo into a ventilated box strapped to the back of a bearer, and set off again down the mountains for the tortuous journey back to Dos Ríos.

The Larsons' unusual and increasing rapport with the Indians, a previously unruly people, did not go unnoticed. One day a government representative stopped by the Dos Ríos hacienda. "Would you be superintendent of schools in the Oriente?" ("Oriente," in Ecuador, means the jungle area east of the mountains.) And later the question came, "Would you supervise road building?" And then, "Will you handle the salt sales?" (A precious commodity for the natives, the government kept a monopoly on the production and distribution of salt in Ecuador.) "Would you set up a meteorological station and send us regular reports? And the gold the Indians are collecting, would you see that it gets to the Banco Central?"

Larson jumped at every opportunity that would bring him into closer contact with these people. Machete in hand, he joined with the Indians as they hacked their way through the jungle, clearing a muddy trail wide enough for a horse to negotiate. Soon this jovial, efficient, politically astute American Swede had earned the nickname "King of the Oriente." Larson's consistent success in everything he tackled won him great acceptance with government officials, and they sought ways to show their appreciation, summoning him to the Presidential Palace for a hearty commendation.

As Larson went about the Oriente, he was constantly seeking new ways to reach out with the gospel. Before coming to Ecuador, Reuben had been exposed in the States to the coming phenomenon of radio; he also had heard about a missionary in Africa who was using some mysterious amplifying system to reach the masses. Remembering the Indians' initial reluctance to come out of the forest, Larson began to visualize a "singing radio" hanging from the branches of a bamboo tree. Would this be the way to get the gospel out to the Indians of the jungle? He began to ponder that this new thing which was sweeping North America would surely reach South America, that someday there would be more receivers. Could they use this new tool, radio, to "reach even further into the darkness"?

The more obstacles
you have,
the more opportunities
there are for God
to do something.
C. W. Jones

Home on furlough, as Reuben and Grace traveled across the
United States presenting their mission work, Reuben often
interjected the possibility of someday using radio for a more
speedy and thorough coverage of the world with the gospel.

One night, while Grace was addressing a gathering of young
people in Omaha, Nebraska, and Reuben was speaking elsewhere, it so happened that Clarence and Katherine were on one
of their "working holidays"—a weekend away from the Tab
but with Clarence assigned to lead the singing at the Omaha
Gospel Tabernacle with Dr. Robert R. Brown.

And thus the Joneses were at the meeting when Grace Larson
spoke. She gave a stirring appeal, and then turned to Clarence,
asking him to take the altar call. Clarence refused: "I'm sorry,
but I'm going to the altar myself."

After the service, the three young people found an ice cream
shop and talked for a couple of hours. It was an excited Grace
who reported to Reuben: "I've met a young man who is
working in gospel radio, and who is so interested in missionary
radio that he already has made a trip to Venezuela to see if he
could establish a station there for South America!"

Finally, in January of 1930, Reuben and Grace Larson came
to the Chicago Tabernacle, and Clarence and Katherine invited

them to stay at their apartment. After the service, little Marian and Marjorie Jones played with Dick and Peggy Larson till they all tumbled off to sleep, bedded down on various couches, while their parents sat around the kitchen table and talked the night away. Ruth and J. D. Clark joined them.

Kath's heart began to be softened. Grace Larson and Ruth Clark were different from any missionaries she had previously known. "They were both so stylish and maintained high standards, with sterling silver and fine bone china even in the jungle."

That night, the hearts of the three men were knit together. At 3 A.M. *they pledged themselves to bring to reality the vision of missionary broadcasting.* In view of the favor Larson enjoyed with the Ecuadorian government, it was agreed that he would return to the field and obtain the permit to broadcast; Jones was to raise funds at home.

Now they also realized that if Reuben and John Clark were to get involved, they must have the blessing of their sponsoring mission, so with some trepidation they arranged to present the proposition of gospel missionary radio to the Christian & Missionary Alliance Annual Conference in Pittsburgh's Carnegie Hall. Many Christians still did not see how this "tool of the devil" could be used for the gospel. Larson, J. D. Clark, and C. W. decided it would be expedient to take up the matter beforehand with the foreign secretary of the C & MA, Dr. Walter Turnbull. Paul Young from Guayaquil had just arrived and he joined in the meeting.

They were elated to discover that Turnbull not only saw the potential of radio, but he had a vision even bigger than their own: "To reach the world with the gospel of Jesus Christ, we need strong transmitters in three locations: the Philippines for the Orient, somewhere in South America for the millions of Spanish and Portuguese there, and in Palestine for Africa and the Moslem world," Turnbull declared. "If you can get into South America, great!" Consequently, not only did they get the approval of the C & MA Council, but their full blessing as they wished Larson "Godspeed" for his safe return to Quito and the securing of a contract with the Ecuadorian government. However, the radio station was not to be under the umbrella of the C & MA.

Before Reuben left for South America, he and C. W. hammered out the proposed contract that among other things would give 20 percent of broadcast time to the government; in return, the fledgling radio station would be exempt from payment of any duty on goods brought into the country for use of the station or its personnel.

Clarence Jones immediately set about the task of raising money for "the world's first missionary radio station."

"The people at the Tab thought he was crazy," Rader's sister recalls. "Jones's folly," they called it. "Set up a radio station to evangelize Ecuador?" they said. "With only six receiving sets in the whole country, who is going to listen to you? It's like putting gasoline stations in a country where there are no automobiles. It just won't work!"

And where was the money going to come from? Very practically, brother-in-law Chet reminded Clarence that the stock market had crashed just a few months earlier (on November 1, 1929) and that America was heading fast into the blackest depression of its history. Hardly an auspicious time to launch a faith mission project dependent on people's freewill giving!

"That could all very well be," said Clarence. "But when you start a work of this kind, everything is an obstacle. And the more obstacles you have, the more opportunities there are for God to do something."

Looking back, Jones sums up: "Here was a tremendous medium—radio—with the twentieth century challenge: 'Go south with the gospel by radio.' It may not have made any sense or logic. From the human standpoint, it may have appeared plain foolhardy. But when for eight years you have watched a man like Paul Rader trust the Lord and go ahead regardless of the circumstances, it seemed the logical thing to do.

"So although it appeared to be poor timing from the economic standpoint, yet it was God's timing, and we're very grateful we happened to be around."

When God's finger points,
God's hand will open the door.
C. W. Jones

10

C. W. liked to quote Jonathan Goforth: " 'God never asked me to do a job but that he sent along men to help me do it.' To launch radio, God sent along Reuben Larson, John and Stuart Clark, and Paul Young."

These missionaries were no strangers to the mighty workings of God, having been exposed to such miracles as the time when coworker Raymond Edman had staggered in from the jungle desperately ill. "He'll be dead by morning," the doctor had advised. Edman's wife dyed her wedding dress black so as to be ready for the funeral, which in the tropics would take place soon after death. But up in Boston, Dr. Joseph Evans interrupted the prayer meeting that night—"I feel we must pray for Ray Edman in Ecuador." The group prayed desperately, until Evans concluded, "Praise the Lord! The victory is won!" Edman recovered, and went on to become president of Wheaton College. (And it was from Wheaton College forty years later that he was promoted to glory as he addressed the students in chapel.)

God had already put Reuben Larson in a place of favor with the Ecuadorian government. However, before any approach could be made, Reuben first had to enlist the support of Stuart (D. S.) Clark, Chairman of the C & MA committee in Ecuador, responsible for twenty-nine workers. (Another six serving

under the Gospel Missionary Union made up the total complement of evangelical missionaries in Ecuador in 1930.)

Again Larson expected opposition, afraid that Clark also
would ask, "With virtually no receiving sets in the country,
how will the people hear?" But instead, D. S. said, "Let's do it!"
and joined hands with Reuben in all approaches to the government.

Stuart Clark, educated in England and Switzerland as were
many high-born Latin Americans, also had won the favor of the
Ecuadorian government and was often an official member of
the "Cometiva" on presidential tours of the Republic. As well,
the Christian and Missionary Alliance lawyer in Quito, Dr. Luis
Calisto, was a man of great influence, an esteemed citizen and
member of the City Council. Calisto had open admiration for
the work that missionaries such as the Clarks and Reuben
Larson were doing. "They have come to help my country." He
would always defend them in the face of criticism. In retrospect,
Stuart would marvel: "God gave us the chance to hold onto
Calisto's coattails as he went in to see the Minister of this or
that—even to the President himself!" Calisto was intrigued with
the prospect of radio in his country. Thus the negotiating of the
contract was put into his capable hands.

And now the miracles started in earnest. "Where God's
finger points, God's hand will open the door," C. W. would
say. In the Ecuadorian system, before any contract could be
presented to the Congress, it first had to be screened by a senior
official. Later this official told Larson of the inner conflict he
had felt as he read through the document proposing a Protestant
radio station. "How can I approve this?" he wondered. The
whole background of Ecuador was one of strong opposition to
all religions other than Roman Catholic.

"But there was something inside me that impelled me to put
my signature on this contract." So he stamped it with his *visto
bueno* and sent it over to the President's office.

In the President's office, the young secretary, Carlos Andrade
Marín, saw this application for a radio station for Ecuador. This
excited him tremendously, and he took it from the bottom of

the pile of papers and put it on top. Andrade Marín did this several times before it finally got the President's attention. At last, the whole Congress voted, and the President signed the bill which permitted these "foreigners and heretics" (as all evangelicals were then classed) to establish the first radio station in Ecuador. "The hearts of kings are in God's hands," Reuben explains simply.

It also could have been that, although the members of Congress realized that by and large the attitude throughout the country might not be favorable, as strong patriots they felt it was right if Ecuador were to move ahead into the twentieth century. "Many of them were open to new things," Reuben said. "Clearly we saw the hand of God moving on the whole Congress of Ecuador, causing them to allow, in this closed Catholic country, a ministry of gospel radio."

On August 15, 1930, the men in Quito flashed off a cable to Jones: "25-year contract granted! Jeremiah 33:3 and Zechariah 4:6! Come!"

But C. W. was already on the way. Absolutely assured that God's hand was moving to open Ecuador's doors, C. W. had booked passage; then he and Katherine parked the children with Aunt Ruth and Uncle Chet and headed for New York and Boston, stopping for services all along the way.

Their old car let them down several times. Once, to Clarence's great mortification, just near Naigara Falls they had to be towed in, and this delayed them from being in Toronto in time for the Peoples Church Wednesday night service—the first meeting C. W. had ever failed to show up for, and he had not been able to reach Oswald Smith by telephone to explain their predicament.

"Can't understand this break in our plans which will embarrass Mr. Smith and certainly chagrins us," Jones recorded in his diary that day. "Another of those places in our experience where we learn that our steps, and stops too, are ordered of the Lord."

The next day tersely records: "Drive on all day toward New York. Must hurry to conclude sailing arrangements since notice has come that boat leaves one day sooner than scheduled. Don't have enough money for tourist rooms, so we will sleep in car parked on a side road."

In New York, Clarence headed straight for the Ecuadorian Consulate and more difficulties. "Find I need more approval on health certificates, vaccination, etc. Go to New York Health Department. At first receive no consideration from clerks, but the Lord fixes it so I meet Assistant Health Director who readily gives me necessary papers. Praise God for this token!" Returning to the Consulate, Clarence had his visa within the hour.

Up in Dudley, some sixty miles southwest of Boston, they had a fine visit with Richard Oliver. Clarence was counting on Richard to handle the music side of the programming for this exciting new missionary venture. In fact, they had hoped that Rich would have gone along on this exploratory trip to Ecuador, but financially it didn't work out for Oliver.

Clarence and Richard drove up to Boston early Sunday morning for Howard Ferrin and Carlton Booth's Mountain Top Hour broadcast over WEAN and WNAC, with the theme song Clarence's "I've Been on the Mountain Top and Seen His Face," written two years earlier on a mountain top in Venezuela, and picked up by Carlton Booth. "Had a precious time of fellowship with dear old Rich. He is a real brother and pal," C. W. recorded that night.

They drove all through Monday night, arriving early in New York for a final flurry of arrangements. By 11:15 A. M. on August 19 they were at the Brooklyn Piers, with Clare's baggage all aboard, and time to give Kath a quick tour of the ship. In his cabin they said their good-byes.

That night Clarence wrote: "Had only a few precious moments with my sweetheart who has borne up so bravely as our last hours together drew near. Surely thank the Lord for such a pal and companion as Kath, who has entered all along so wholeheartedly into our acceptance of God's challenge for our lives and the plan of radio broadcasting for South America. It will mean so much to her to have to go home alone to break it up and take smaller place. I am praying the Lord to give her added strength and courage as I leave.

"Whistles blowing! Bells ringing! At eight bells everybody's ashore who's not sailing. Soon we're slipping away from the wharf, loved ones, home, the good old U.S.A. There they stand— waving to us till we can't see them anymore. God be with you, dearest, till we meet again."

And he shall be
as the light of the morning,
when the sun riseth,
even a morning
without clouds....
2 *Samuel* 23:4

John and Ruth Clark were returning from furlough on the same ship, and so the twelve days at sea passed quickly. They went through the Panama Canal and finally dropped anchor in the harbor of Guayaquil where Clarence shared a room with veteran missionary H.V. Chrisman; Chrisman and William Reid had been in the late 1890s the first two evangelical missionaries to enter Ecuador. And here in Guayaquil Clarence had his first real introduction to South American timetables— quite a learning experience for a man who cannot tolerate tardiness and always wears his watch on the inside of his wrist, especially when he's reading a radio script, so that it could be instantly visible.

"This is the land of mañana for sure. The auto truck we are to take at 7 A.M. does not get away until 9:30," he recorded one day. The next day C.W. noted: "We've missed two trains lately, so not to be fooled today, we arrive at 4 A.M. to catch the 4:30 train. It finally pulls in at 5:15, and doesn't leave till after 6:00."

Another day: "We're up early, but miss the launch to Duran . . . have to hire special launch, but still arrive too late for train. John Clark secures permission for us to be taken by hand car upon payment of first-class passage. Away we go at 1:00 P.M., clicking along the rails through fertile plains and heavy plantation growths. Some trip! Can't get over being pumped along in this ludicrous fashion, seated on a park bench at the front end of a hand car."

Then the diary goes on: "Great service in the plaza at night. Played [trombone] and showed pictures. This little projector is a whiz." (He'd brought down the latest model to show stereopticon slides.) "John spoke. Several came back to the church to learn more about the Way. Praise God for the chance to tell the story to over 500 nationals."

On another out-trip: "Visit several believers, play and sing for them. After five miles horseback ride to Venice, we miss the train. Drunken *camion* drivers [a camion was a truck with a few seats for passengers] cannot get us back, so we have to make trip to Milagro on horseback—some job when they have to be prodded at each step. Hold service in a little second story room with a handful of folks and a heartful of blessing."

The innovative Clarence had also brought along a 16 mm. movie camera, quite a novelty in 1930. From the heckling he'd already taken about this "scatterbrained, foolhardy project," he knew he would have to have promotion strong enough to override all objections. So he determined to capture "living" pictures. At every opportunity he was rolling film. "Sneak away to shoot some movies of a bullfight," he recorded one Sunday afternoon. "My, what some of these dear missionaries would think if they knew I had been in that arena for any cause!"

In Guayaquil, Clarence happened to meet a team of engineers from an American radio manufacturer who had just finished researching the possibilities of broadcasting in Ecuador. "There's no way," they told him. "Ecuador has too many mountains. The high mineral content with its strong magnetic force will seriously weaken, absorb, or scramble any signal hopelessly. Whatever you do, stay away from the mountains!"

Clarence's heart sank, because only a month earlier he had been in Washington checking with the State Department as to the best place in Ecuador to locate a radio station. "Ecuador?

Reception conditions are nil. You must get away from the equator. We would suggest you avoid Ecuador altogether," they advised.

Avoid Ecuador! But they were committed. They'd signed a contract with the government pledging to broadcast daily, and he and Larson were planning to purchase property for the station. Yet according to these reports by the experts, it seemed as if Ecuador was just about the worst place on earth they could put a station.

And particularly Quito. "Stay away from the mountains; get as far away from the equator as you can," they had said. Quito, situated at 9,300 feet was completely surrounded by mountains, and only fifteen miles south of the equator!

Maybe they should consider locating the station in Guayaquil. It was farther away from the equator, and at sea level. As well, the church was more established than in Quito. As the port of entry, Guayaquil was certainly the commercial center for Ecuador. There was much in its favor.

Clarence walked along beside the broad Guayas River in Guayaquil's warm tropical night, the humidity pressing in. In spite of all he had heard, his "Divine Radar" was at work. "Come up to the top of the mountain" was ringing in his head and heart, the call of God to his servant Moses.

"Come up to the mountain? When all these engineers tell us we're crazy to even be in Ecuador, let alone in Quito? Is this really what you are saying?"

"Come up to the top of the mountain. Call unto me and I will show you great and mighty things." It was a refrain that there was no mistaking. And what was Reuben's verse? "Not by might, nor by power, but by my Spirit."

Unreasonable, illogical though it seemed, Clarence was absolutely certain that Quito was God's place for his voice to South America. But this was a matter they must all be sure of: Reuben, Stuart and John Clark, and Paul Young.

Before Clarence left Guayaquil, he had worked out a deal with two local Christian businessmen, John and Alan Reed, that if C.W. would come through with daily radio programming, they would import and sell radio receivers throughout Ecuador. Another obstacle removed!

The train trip from Guayaquil to Quito is rated as one of the most exciting and scenic in the world. To board the train, you cross by launch to the south shore of the Guayas River. In spite of a 4:30 A.M. start, Clarence's trunks somehow were put on the wrong launch and just barely got onto the train as they pulled out of the station at 7:30 A.M. for the two-day trip over the Andes Mountains. As the little train chugged its way up through the tropical forest, past tall palm trees and the lacy fern of bamboo, with frothy waterfalls cascading down the mountainside, Clarence was leaning out the window, shooting movies.

The little engine took a rest before climbing the Devil's Nose, a dizzying engineering marvel with gouged-out track, zig-zagging up the sheer rock face which drops a thousand feet straight down into the canyon. Slowly the train inches its way up the mountain wall, coming to a halt on a siding; then it begins to back up the next stretch of track, again coming to a halt on a siding; forward again. Up, up the little train climbs, 10,000 feet in fifty miles.

At 11,800 feet Clarence found himself above the clouds, rattling around curves through the cold bleak lands of "The Paramo" where only a few Quichua Indians tend sheep and grow a little grain. Right across the top of the Andes they clattered and swerved. Through breaks in the clouds, as far as he could see on both sides of the train, peak after peak marched away to the horizon. In late afternoon they came to mighty "old Chimborazo," a magnificent snowcapped volcano, the tallest peak in Ecuador, soaring 20,709 feet into the azure sky.

In Quito, D. S. Clark and Clarence met with Señor Luis Calisto, the lawyer who had worked out the final details of the radio contract. "Find all arrangements OK," Clarence reported. "I'm delighted with the marvelous way the Lord has undertaken for us in this project." "Quito, this ancient, glorious capital of Ecuador, is a great city," he noted on his first visit. "I like its people, its beauty, its progressive air. The climate is wonderfully fresh and invigorating."

Clarence was anxious to visit Reuben and Grace, and to see the territory so he'd have an idea of the Indians and the jungle country when they started radio programs and distributing radio sets later. "D. S. tells me the journey will be hard. We must pack all food and plenty of blankets, as nights are cool and the country is absolutely desolate and uninhabited. Plan to retire early, but 11 P.M. finds me reading and writing home." Even so, the next day Jones records in his diary that he and Stuart Clark rose at 1:30 A.M. for an early breakfast.

"Take auto to beginning of horse trail two hours from Quito. Ride away into beautiful moonlight, down fantastic trail, through lanes of eucalyptus trees and eerie shadows. The sunrise at 6:00 A.M. is beautiful—gold touching snowy volcanic peaks to right and behind us. Through the Paramo in two hours of snow, sleet, hail, and rain. Rubber ponchos are a godsend.

"Muleteer, a sierra Indian, trudges ahead on foot, prodding along our two cargo mules. Steep, rugged, stony, muddy trail—up, up, up; down, down, down. Paramo is cold, barren tableland between Andes peaks, often with no trail. Finally start dropping down. Reach crystal lake for lunch time; eat in a drizzle of rain.

"Push on after very few minutes; getting saddle stiff. The glorious mountain scenery makes one forget incidental discomforts. During this trip of some 250 miles we go up over Paramo at 13,500, then drop 12,000 feet into jungle. Going into Dos Ríos will take two days by horseback, three days hike, and another day by horse—if we make good time. And then we have to come out again. By air—only seventy-five miles or one hour's flying time!"

Day two: "...the trail is rough and very hard to follow because of landslides, washouts...."

Day three: "With our four Indians ahead bearing boxes and bags, we start out on long hike. Climbing, pushing, pulling, sliding, trudging—this trail through the Oriente is hard work. I marvel at these Indians' endurance. I'm very tired. Find I have overestimated my strength. Stu has to help me along, and calls back Indians to build native 'tambo' for the night. Out of bamboo, green withes, and leaves, they soon build us a snug little shelter. Wet mud floor, but then, what's that when one is dead tired!"

On day nine they finally arrived at Dos Ríos, "a gem carved out of the jungle," only to find that the Larsons had started out for Quito and the Annual Missionary Alliance Conference just two days earlier, taking a longer but easier route over the mountains through Baños and Ambato.

Out at Dos Ríos Clarence got some splendid movie footage of shooting jungle rapids in dugout canoe. At one point, on an impulse he handed the camera bag to his "camera boy" asking him to carry it on land around a treacherous section of the river. Their canoe capsized in the churning rapids, and Clarence's only thought as he was being swept swiftly along was, "Thank goodness, the films weren't in the canoe!"

On the trail back to Quito, Clarence tells of halting the whole procession at one dramatically beautiful spot. Just as he focused the camera, the sun shone to illuminate the vista of rugged slopes and canyons. It was the only five minutes of sunshine in two days. "Happenchance?" he wrote. "I choose to believe God's hand of blessing was on the filming of these missionary moving pictures!"

View your pressures
no longer as burdens,
but as a platform
for his glorious sufficiency!
C. W. Jones

Back in Quito, Clarence officially was to direct the music at the Conference; but more importantly, it was here, when the missionaries—Reuben Larson, Stuart and John Clark, Paul Young, and C. W.—were sitting around informally that someone asked, "What are we going to call this new radio station?"

The international call letters assigned to Ecuador were "HC." These would have to be at the beginning of the final series of call letters. Larson and Jones, both keen promoters, asked, "Can we come up with some kind of slogan?" Someone else said, "It should be in Spanish because that is what most of our programming will be."

"How about Hoy Cristo?" Stuart suggested.

"Hoy Christo Jesús Bendice," Larson said. ("Today Jesus Christ Blesses.")

HCJB had a nice ring to it. Could they find an English slogan to fit as well?

"Heralding Christ Jesus' Blessings!" And they had it. The date was October 3, 1930.

As well, they had to consider how they should respond to the reports of the experts discouraging any radio in Ecuador at all, let alone in Quito. "There is one big advantage to Quito," the men decided. "This is the seat of government. It will be good for us to operate right under their noses so they'll be able to see for themselves exactly what we are doing. Quito it will be."

"After all, radio is to be the new missionary," Clarence reminded them. "Surely we can trust our God to do a new thing, to make a way in the wilderness."

Back in Chicago, supported by faithful prayer warriors from the Gospel Tabernacle, Katherine was desperately seeking to know God's will for South America. One of these prayer warriors, Agnes Cooper, would send over one of her older children to babysit so Kath could slip over for a few minutes of prayer, four or five times a week. As well, Mrs. Cooper spent at least an hour every morning and evening "praying HCJB into existence." Louise Genn's Tabernacle prayer group, which held all-night prayer meetings once or twice a month, was also praying with Kath. Adam Welty was up at 4:00 A.M. each morning crying out for God's guidance in this new undertaking.

Clarence spent the rest of his time in Quito searching for a suitable site, without success. Yet he was rejoicing: "Praise God for victory. He is surely working upon these government men to open doors for us. Praying much, and trusting God for the exact place for the station, and for necessary funds to get home. Six hundred dollars needed."

Quite miraculously, Reuben happened to have $600, no small sum for a missionary to have in hand in 1930. Thus on October 20, Jones set sail for New York.

On October 22, while C. W. was at sea, Richard Oliver was killed in a car accident.

Jones arrived home to the devastating news. (For years he mourned, feeling the loss acutely.) There was also a letter waiting for him: he had been replaced at the Tab. And there was a bill enclosed, for $2000 to cover costs of C. W.'s transportation, and caring for his family during his two-and-one-half-month absence!

Back in Chicago, Jones was staggered by these blows. He had lost his best friend. He had no job. He'd been slapped with a bill for $2000, and he was flat broke.

Clarence went to Paul Rader and found that, yes, he had been replaced, and the bill for $2000 would stand. With a deepening depression, finances at the Tab were tight. Clarence was totally on his own, with no plans, nowhere to turn.

Clinging to "their sustaining rock," Jeremiah 33:3, "Call unto me, and I will answer thee, and show thee great and mighty things," C. W. fell before the Lord. He was absolutely certain that God miraculously had opened the door for missionary broadcasting in Ecuador. But right now, here in the United States they needed desperately for the Lord "to open the way before them." Louise Genn's prayer group at the Tab rallied round, praying the night through.

The very next day, Clarence received a long distance phone call, from Dr. Gerald Winrod of Oklahoma City. Would Clarence come and help him in the new Tabernacle and radio work? Jones was on the next plane.

In early December, he wrote to his friends in Quito: "Dr. Winrod has kindly consented to back our project to the limit, letting us use the Tabernacle as headquarters for the Southwest while we endeavor to secure the necessary funds for our equipment and support. He has also asked me to take a place on the board of the 'Defenders Movement' to represent South America. This has been the first tangible move on the part of the Lord toward the fulfillment of our dreams for radio station HCJB. Our hearts and faces are set towards Ecuador, and when God moves us with our equipment, we shall be on the way in a hurry." (He was also able to enclose a repayment check for Reuben's loan.)

The move to Oklahoma City proved to be a good one. C. W.'s old pal from the brass quartet days, Jimmy Neilson, was directing the band and radio ministry. As well as being introduced to a host of new friends in Oklahoma City, Winrod allowed C. W. to use his mailing list, thus opening the door to even more resources, prayers, and gifts. Winrod ran a series of articles in the *Defender* magazine, "respectfully suggesting that readers in their prayerful tithing should include this faith pioneer radio project which has tremendous possibilities."

In the April 1931 issue of the *Defender* Jones eloquently described the need and the plan:

Our whole creed of service is "Use everything we can that God has given us in this Twentieth Century to speed the taking of the First Century Message." Thus we restate Paul's challenge: "By all means save some."

Even though Satan may have captured a good many devices, we can still reclaim them for Jesus' glory—cleansing them in consecrated usefulness and setting them apart to help us witness better to others of the saving grace of Christ.

Thank God for the many advanced methods that today are at the missionary's disposal. Radio Station HCJB with its 5000 watts on shortwave is in itself a most revolutionary step forward in missionary endeavour. This step calls for kindred steps all along the line as we seek to develop the many possibilities before us.

Howard Ferrin, another buddy from Moody days, promoted Clarence and HCJB at every opportunity at Providence Bible Institute in Rhode Island. Dr. Walter Turnbull proved to be an invaluable friend and advisor, as did Bob Brown of the Omaha Christian Tabernacle.

But then one day Clarence hired a pilot and flew into Omaha with a second-hand Stinson Voyager. (Jones could see no sense in slogging for nine days over mountains and through jungles when you could fly it in an hour. "That is not good logistics," C.W. would say.) Bob Brown sat down for a long talk with Clarence. "C. W., it's too much. First you are trying to sell the Christian public on *radio*, which many still think of as the devil's tool; you are showing *movies* of Ecuador, and for some this again is of the devil; now you go and get an *airplane*. Certainly it's a sensation and you're getting a lot of press. But the Christian public is just not ready for this kind of promotion.

"Clarence, what is it God had called you to do—radio? Then ditch the aircraft. Someone else will take it up. In the meantime, you walk to the jungle. *Where you have purging and pruning, you have greater growth, even though for the moment you have less branches.*"

Jones ditched the aircraft. "This one thing have I desired from the Lord and that will I seek after . . ." was burned into C. W.'s soul from then on. Although willing to "wing it alone," to fly against all human wisdom when the "Divine Radar" so ordered, Clarence valued the judgment and counsel of godly men. He was not a loner, but rather sought out and gathered around him wise men of outstanding ability. "Jones was totally believable. He convinced you that he was able to deliver the goods he was promising. And he always did," lifetime coworkers agree.

Early in the HCJB promotion campaign, Katherine's Uncle Ben Welty, a lawyer and former congressman, had called Clarence aside. "Clare, if you are going to take people's money, you'll want to handle those funds properly, and you'll have to be able to give a receipt. For this you need a legal corporation."

What would they call it? Jones and Larson had discussed this: "We wanted the word 'fellowship' in there, to include the different kinds of people, the different churches, the different backgrounds, all fellowshipping around Christ and around the idea of broadcasting, because there weren't too many people in those days who believed in gospel radio, let alone missionary radio. And as well, we visualized a worldwide outreach.

"What we finally came up with was certainly a mouthful," Clarence admits: "The World Radio Missionary Fellowship, WRMF," incorporated March 9, 1931, in the library of the rescue mission in Lima, Ohio. Clarence Jones was the first president; Adam Welty, his father-in-law, stood in as treasurer, with sister-in-law Ruth Churchill as secretary. Lance and Virginia Latham, brother Howard, and Reuben Larson completed the first board.

Grandmother Detbrener gave the first dollar. "I don't rightly understand what it's all about, but I'm with you, dear ones," she encouraged. Clarence and Kath treasured that first dollar bill, replacing it with one from their own pocket.

Then another remarkable thing happened. At the Chicago Tabernacle, it was the Missions Secretary who had levied the $2000 charge against the Joneses. "He was an ultraconservative who didn't see how radio could fit into missions," Clarence explained. But somehow the Lord turned him completely around, so that when a legacy came into the Tab "to be applied wherever they felt it was most needed in missions," Christian Eicher called Clarence. "Today I've used a $2000 legacy to wipe out your account. God bless you both in this venture." (From that day till now, the Eichers have sent regular support to the Jones family.) For Katherine, this was the final proof that God was working to move them to Ecuador, that truly he was opening the door. Wholeheartedly, she decided that with C. W. she would step through it.

"We felt like a cork that had been weighted to a stone suddenly bobbing to the surface," Clarence relates. "We were fairly bouncing with joy that the Lord had made this wonderful provision so now we were in the clear. We had a sense of being carried along by something greater than ourselves. The most wonderful thing of all is that you don't know what God is doing. Later on, the years have revealed far more than we ever dreamed.

"If God had suddenly shown us everything he was going to do in the years to come, I would have said, 'Wait a minute, you've got the wrong man! In spite of all your wonderful power, you'll have to have somebody who can trust you far more than I can.'

"But God inched up the curtain just a little bit at a time and said, 'Take a look, and take a step.'

"And so we've gone on believing God for what we could see, and we didn't get too frightened until the next step. Then we started all over again, trusting in God's marvelous provision."

In late August of 1931, Clarence departed from the Chicago Gospel Tabernacle, going to South America under the Worldwide Christian Couriers, with Rader's full blessing. At the farewell service Clarence set the new radio transmitter on the platform—not the 5000-watt voice he had promoted, but a puny 250-watt transmitter about four feet high. "Still, it looked pretty impressive, set against the backdrop of a typical Ecuadorian scene that Clarence had painted with mountains and a thatched roof

Indian hut," some of the folks recalled of that occasion.

Paul Rader dedicated Clarence, Katherine, and the transmitter to the ministry of missionary radio in South America. Then taking off his diamond-chip cufflinks, he handed them to Clarence. "These will serve as a link between you and me. God bless you, dear Clarence, if not to India, then to Ecuador."

On the way home that evening, Rader's daughter, Harriet, was upset: "Daddy, why did you send Clarence to South America when he is so talented and so needed here?" And Rader replied, *"You always give the Lord the best for the mission field, the cream of young manhood."*

All we have needed
thy hand hath provided:
Great is thy faithfulness!
Thomas O. Chisholm

Even though Clarence was off to Ecuador to stay, once again he
was traveling without Katherine. They were expecting another
baby in early December, and not having been told that there was
a fine, Vienna-trained obstetrician in Quito, they decided it was
best for Kath to remain in Chicago for the birth.

Still, with all the radio equipment, C. W. had an immense
amount of baggage—thirty-three boxes weighing 6400 pounds,
including the handsome grandfather clock Clarence had bought
for Katherine their second Christmas together. In New York
the shipping agent laughed when he saw the designation, "World
Radio Missionary Fellowship." "Where do you get this 'world'
stuff?" he asked. "With a 250-watt transmitter, you've got to be
kidding!"

Jones was taking with him a brilliant radio technician, Eric
Williams, and Eric's wife, Ann. Eric had been assigned to the
Chicago Tabernacle by CBS as the engineer for their programs
over WBBM, and before long this young scoffer was sitting
with Clarence on a Sunday afternoon and accepting the Lord
Jesus into his heart. The young engineer and his wife caught the
vision, and they too now were going out as part of Rader's
"Worldwide Christian Couriers" team, taking the transmitter
Eric had built in his Chicago garage, to join forces with the
missionaries in Ecuador.

At Guayaquil, Clarence and Eric held their breath as they watched their packing crates being tossed into the launch, then dropped onto the dock and thrown into the Customs shed, where they had quite a time getting it all passed. "They'd never seen equipment like this before," Jones explained. Their transmitter was dumped aboard another launch, bumped onto the train, and banged about on buses and trucks—fifteen times in all their precious cargo was loaded and unloaded, until at last it was delivered, miraculously undamaged with only one trunk missing, to "Quinta Cornston." This was the site chosen for the Pioneer Radio Broadcaster—"HCJB, The Voice of the Andes," which was to be a sister station to Chicago Tabernacle's WJBT (Where Jesus Blesses Thousands").

Reuben Larson had managed to rent, with option to purchase, a reasonably priced compound the size of four city blocks, with quite a nice house. Now came the challenge to construct the radio station—a first for world missions and for Ecuador. Basically, they'd need a studio and control room, a transmitter building, towers and an antenna.

The studio and control room was simple: Jones cut a hole through the two-foot-thick adobe wall of their living room to an adjoining "Florida Room" sun porch, and set in a glass panel. There were two switches in the control room, one for the microphone and one for the phonograph. For better acoustics, an old-fashioned carbon-model microphone was suspended by "hair-curler" springs from a circular piece of metal and housed inside the "cavern," as they called the two-by-four-foot packing case in which the transmitter had been shipped down, lined with red velvet from Clarence's mother's old living room drapes. "Actually, it sounded as if we were in a barrel," Clarence remembers.

As for the transmitter site, right in the middle of the compound the previous owner had built a shed for his thoroughbred sheep. It wasn't much of a place, just two mud walls with a corrugated, galvanized tin roof. Jones and an Indian helper walled up the open sides with adobe brick, poured a cement floor, whitewashed the whole thing, and brought in that "mighty whisper of the Andes." "All 250 watts could sit on one table," Jones recalls. "The first night it rained on the tin roof, I thought they'd let loose with all the Howitzers in the U. S. Navy. Then the hail came, and that was worse!"

To support the antenna, Jones had grandly envisioned stately steel towers, and this is what he had pictured on their first letterhead. "But instead we wound up by going to the telephone company and asking if we could have a couple of their tallest poles."

When these eighty-five-foot eucalyptus poles came down the side street beside. Quinta Cornston, "they looked longer than the Eiffel Tower" to the excited missionaries. With holes dug in the ground and guy wires to secure the base, the missionaries attached pulleys at the top of the poles; then, with all of the Indians they could commandeer off the street, they pushed the two "towers" into an upright position, 200 feet apart.

But now came the problem: How were they to fasten the antenna wire to the top of these poles? Little Pedro, the gardener's son, supplied the solution. For one *sucre*, he shinnied up one pole, then the second pole, with a rope in his teeth, and he threaded the ends through the pulleys. Tied to the rope ends was HCJB's first antenna—a straight horizontal wire stretched 200 feet from pole to pole, eighty-five feet off the ground.

Jones and Williams measured and remeasured that wire to a fine exactness to ensure proper tuning at 50.26 meters, or 5986 kilocycles. Again, as Ecuador's first radio station, they'd had the choice of location on the dial. "We'll take dead center where we can't be missed," they had decided.

The target date for the first broadcast was Christmas Day, 1931. From December 1 on, the two men "ate and slept that little transmitter." By Christmas Eve, all was purring nicely. Suddenly, there was a sickening silver-blue fizzle. "Our last power tube has blown!" Williams cried. "All our spares are in that missing trunk."

There was only one man in the whole country who might have the tube they needed (a blue mercury power rectifier). Clare jumped into the car and roared off for Riobamba and

Carlos Córdovez—Ecuador's only ham operator. The 120 miles were long ones on 1931 roads—the trip took at least six hours—but C. W. finally got back to Quito with the tube that Córdovez graciously had taken from his set and loaned to Jones, just in time for the scheduled broadcast to go on.

(Right after Christmas, Williams and Jones once more went down to the freight depot. There was the missing trunk, but all identifying papers had been removed! "Lord, loose this trunk for us," C. W. prayed as Eric dickered with the clerks. Just then, an official walked into the baggage room, and very quickly they had their trunk!)

By mid-afternoon on Christmas Day, the Pioneer Missionary Broadcaster group had all gathered in the Quinta Cornston living room: Clarence, Grace and Reuben Larson, Stuart and Erma Clark, John and Ruth Clark, plus Edna Figg and Ruth Popejoy who were from the C & MA school. Out in the shed Eric Williams was praying as he switched on the transmitter—there'd been no time to test the borrowed tube. Ann Williams was at the controls.

All eyes were on the big grandfather clock. As the hands approached 3:00 P.M. on this historic Friday, December 25, 1931, Clarence hushed the children, then poked his head inside the "cavern" toward the elaborately rigged microphone: "Hoy Cristo Jesús Bendice!" On the old portable organ Ruth Clark struck up the first notes, pumping furiously in an attempt to hide the tap-tapping of the footpedals as the bellows was losing air, while Clarence played on his trombone what was to become HCJB's glorious signature hymn, "Great Is Thy Faithfulness."

Then it was Reuben's turn to lean into the microphone and say: "Esta es la Voz de los Andes, Radiodifusora HCJB" (This is the Voice of the Andes, HCJB") and from that day on there would be daily programming, in Spanish. Erma Clark and Edna Figg sang. John Clark delivered the first prayer, D. S. brought a brief message in English, and then Reuben Larson preached, for the first time sending the gospel of Christ over the airwaves to listeners in a foreign land. There was a grand total of thirteen receiving sets in all of Ecuador, and the people who owned them had been alerted.

Out in the sheepshed, for thirty tense minutes Eric nursed along the homemade transmitter, hoping desperately that they were on the air. And indeed they were. Right after the program, the handcranked telephone rang, first one caller, then another, congratulating and thanking HCJB for this wondrous event.

All the missionaries in Quito gathered in Quinta Cornston for a Christmas feast—sixteen adults and twelve children—to enjoy "two turkeys (eighty cents each), two chickens, and all the 'fixins' which could be secured."

"Best of all was the fellowship with each other," Clare wrote home to Kath. "After the meal, we had games for the children and grownups until we were exhausted with fun; then we had a most delightful prayer service to end the gathering. It was a very, very precious time because we sensed that God was doing something new, something wonderful, something we couldn't even describe. We had a sense that God was in it."

Those who could stay on helped to broadcast a simple Christmas night program in English. They sang a few carols, Clarence again played, they had several solos, and Stuart Clark gave a short message. After the half hour the phone rang again, with English-speaking listeners telling how they had sat by their receivers and cried during the whole program.

"It's a peculiar thrill to stand back of the microphone here and realize that we are actually beginning the blessed work to which we have looked forward so long," Clarence wrote home. "The big thing that so encouraged us was that folks like the Larsons and the Clarks who had been in traditional missionary work for so many years were amongst the very first to be captivated by this, the great vision, the great imagination—that God could do something in the air. It's the answer to the prayers and gifts of a handful of friends in the homeland. It's God's answer to his promise in Jeremiah 33:3 and Zechariah 4:6. It is the start of Heralding Christ Jesus Blessings. We remembered that the Lord had really begun broadcasting 1900 years before at Bethlehem with an angel choir singing, 'Emmanuel—God with us.' And we hoped that this beginning of missionary radio overseas would re-echo the same lovely story of the Christchild, His death and resurrection. It is all His doing—and glorious in our eyes. Hoy Cristo Jesús Bendice!"

Clarence Jones was high on the mountain top that night. "But you never stay there," he reminds. "There are more valleys than mountain peaks. You learn that in the Andes."

We cannot do
our work alone.
We must do it
together,
and we must do it
as colleagues.
C. W. Jones

14

After all had left and Quinta Cornston was quiet, Clarence was writing long into the night, to Katherine who was still in Chicago, and to his little family, now numbering three. Katherine had gone to Grant Hospital late in the evening of December 12. Thinking he had a little time to kill, her doctor had stepped across the road for a cup of coffee, and when he returned, the hospital gates were locked. He pounded and shouted and rang the bell, but could not get in. Up in the delivery room, the birth had speeded up, and the nurses were getting frantic. Finally the security guard made rounds and found the furious doctor still pounding on the gates. He rushed upstairs, and just after midnight on December 13, delivered Richard Wesley Jones. (Clarence received the cablegram on his thirty-first birthday on December 15, 1931.)

Katherine spent a weepy Christmas Day in the little apartment with the children, finally putting away Clare's photograph because she couldn't stand to look at it, so great was her ache of loneliness. Across the miles, Clarence reached out to his new son with this poignant little poem:

My Boy

Dear little fellow—newcomer, dear,
Welcome you are, and cherished here;
Sorry I was not there the day
You came into our lives to stay
  Bringing us joy—
  My little boy!

For my absence I apologize;
Really it couldn't be otherwise—
Else I'd been there by your mother's side;
Couldn't help much, but then I'd have tried
  Singing for joy!
  My little boy.

When will I see your tiny face?
When can I take your daddy's place?
When will your hand my heart caress?
Not for a long time still, I guess.
  Bundle of joy
  My little boy.

We've called you Richard Wesley, son,
One was my pal's name—mine is one,
Just be like him—you'll make me glad—
Welcome! my son, from your far away Dad.
  Promise of joy,
  My little boy.

December 1931

Just as Katherine was planning to sail, Marian came down with whooping cough; then, when Marian was almost well, Marjorie succumbed. So the weeks dragged on. Finally, with all recovered, Katherine was getting anxious. In early April, Rader called from Los Angeles where he was having meetings: "Katherine, I think it's time for you to leave for Quito. Come as soon as you can."

Quickly Katherine packed and traveled by train to the coast with Marian, not quite seven, Marjorie almost five, and the three-and-a-half-month-old Richard. (Kath herself was not yet twenty-eight.)

Rader put Katherine aboard the Panama-bound ship with twenty-one pieces of luggage, plus a baby carriage for Richard, and two doll carriages.

"You can't take these little girls to a foreign land without doll carriages!" Aunt Ruth had insisted as she trundled off the family heirlooms. Kath also had with her five gallons of sterile water, a year's supply of SMA formula powder, and a big carton of the brand-new disposable diapers.

The steward led Katherine to her cabin. When he started down the ladder toward the steerage quarters, Kath was appalled. "I can't possibly manage that ladder with these two girls and a baby. Isn't there something else?" "I'm sorry, but steerage is all that is left. But I'll check."

And yes, there was something else—a cabin right across from the dining room, and the girls could be part of the first-class entertainment program, which en route included a marvelous birthday party for Marian.

When they arrived in Panama where they were to wait for a boat to Ecuador, a fellow passenger from the Bible Society, learning that Kath had less than ten dollars, took the young mother around Panama looking for a cheap hotel. But in vain. "The best place for you to stay here is the Tivoli," he advised.

Holding her head high, the young Mrs. Jones approached the desk in this fine hotel and asked to see the manager. "I have no money and no passport. However, they are both in the mail for me." (Rader had promised to forward them to Panama.)

"But I know your husband," the manager beamed. "Sometimes on my radio I have been able to hear HCJB," and he gave her the key to a sumptuous suite.

For ten days Katherine watched for the mail. Nothing. The next day they should be sailing for Ecuador. How would she pay her hotel bill? "Mrs. Jones, I shall gladly go bond for you, and you can pay me when you get the money," the manager offered gallantly. But the very day of sailing, the money and passport arrived. With an overflowing heart Kath went aboard, and she even had twenty-five dollars left for pocket money.

The girls looked their finest—their starched dresses flouncing, their white shoes sparkling. Kath asked the stewardess to mind them while she checked their quarters. Down, down they went to the lowest part of steerage, which had no running water! "But I can't stay here," she protested. "I knew you couldn't as soon as I saw you," the booking agent agreed. "How much money can you afford to pay for better quarters?" Kath had the twenty five dollars which she thought was a rather grand sum. "Madam, it would cost $250. But there is a room on the upper deck I shall let you have." So once again Katherine and the children had a luxurious voyage.

The boat came upriver and anchored off Guayaquil at midnight on May 21, 1932. They had been traveling for six weeks from Chicago. Kath stood by the rail looking across the black water to the lights of the city. "Clarence is there somewhere!"

There was no sleep that night for an excited Katherine. At 5 A.M. they were up while Kath dressed and undressed the girls several times, fixing them their prettiest for Daddy. People began to come aboard and they would hear footsteps approaching their cabin: "There's Daddy!" But Daddy did not come. Finally all the passengers were off and the ship was unloaded. The captain turned to a tearful Katherine: "I'm sorry, but you really must leave the ship. We have to head back for Panama immediately. Go to the Reed Brothers. They'll look after you," he said, and he handed Kath down the ladder into the launch that would take her to shore.

Two weeks earlier, Clarence had been out in the jungle at Dos Ríos when his built-in sense of timing that tells him when it's time to go or stop, regardless of anything or anyone else—this "Divine Radar" told him "Katherine is coming." (Clarence knew that Katherine was en route, but he did not know her exact date of arrival.) Clarence hurried to Guayaquil and found that indeed a boat was due in, but not for two days. Furthermore, Katherine's name was not on the passenger list. Still, Clarence was absolutely certain that Katherine's arrival was imminent.

Determined to meet his sweetheart in style, Clarence arranged for a private launch, and then went to a friend's place to spend the night. He couldn't know that even then Kath's boat was steaming upriver.

Right after breakfast the next day, Clarence became uneasy. He checked once more. "There's no way that boat will be in before tomorrow," he was told. Yet something impelled him to head for the docks, and there was a ship in the harbor—Katherine's—ahead of time.

From the little launch chugging towards the shore, Katherine saw the love of her life standing on the pier, and what a reunion, after nine agonizingly long months. But when Katherine told him that they had been waiting, wondering, disappointed, for hours, Clare could not forgive himself. When he had had the intuition to come out of the jungle to meet Kath, why then did he not know to come to the harbor sooner and so spare his beloved such an ordeal? He'd gone to the trouble of hiring the launch, yet the timing was off. He'd tried so hard, and still he had let his family down.

When you broadcast
to people of another language
or culture—
use *their* dictionary.
Carl Lawrence

The warm hospitality of Christians in Guayaquil soon banished Katherine's frightening introduction to Ecuador.

The train ride to Quito enthralled the children and Katherine, exhausting though it was. Then, when Clarence drove them up the curving maple-lined driveway into Quinta Cornston, their new Ecuadorian home, they could not believe the charming ivy-covered English cottage set in a two-and-half-acre park of eucalyptus trees and formal gardens, with magnolias and bougainvillea, lilies and roses in profusion, apple and peach trees trained against the wall enclosing the whole Quinta.

Once inside the front door, Katherine was immediately aware of the problem that had been bothering Clarence ever since his arrival—the floors. Originally a yellow-painted board, they had been rubbed with repeated applications of floor wax and crude oil to a mucky, tacky finish that stuck to your feet at every step.

After a few weeks, when Katherine still did not have the floors scrubbed clean, Clarence let her know he was disappointed. "Do you realize what a large area there is?" Kath retorted. "I've tried, and nothing works on this mess."

Clare just had to wait until Kath got a letter back from her stepmother: "Try Red Seal Lye." She and Pedro went at a small hall first, sloshing the solution over the floor and letting it soak overnight, being careful that Pedro didn't burn his bare feet. It was a big job, but finally Kath and Pedro had it licked.

In the kitchen in the place of a refrigerator, Katherine had a *guardafrio*—a box in the window with screening all around As an extra precaution, Kath boiled the milk afternoons as well as mornings. For milk delivery, the cow came to the door; Kath would take out her pail and the local dairy farmer would milk a pailful on the doorstep. The government discovered that some less honorable milk merchants had a balloon full of water up their sleeve and they would slyly be squirting water into the pail along with the milk. So that ended door delivery.

The stove was a big British wood-burning model. When Katherine tried to bake cakes and pies, they just would not cook. Then she discovered that she had to build a fire on the top, at the sides and underneath the oven. The children remember the wonderful smell of drying apples after they were sliced and strung on long strings across the kitchen; the sauerkraut ripening in big barrels; the pots of corned beef. "The Quinta Cornston was a fantastic place to be a child," the youngsters recall, "with rabbits and ponies, and dogs having litters, and cats having kittens on the beds. We'd play Tarzan, swinging from pine tree to pine tree."

Smack in the middle of all this family commotion, Clarence was running a radio station in a studio off the living room, with speakers and singers constantly coming and going. Handicapped at first by his lack of proficiency in Spanish, Jones hired a Spanish announcer as soon as possible, but had to rely heavily on resident missionaries for the radio ministry. Reuben came up from Dos Ríos as often as he could; Paul Young was a frequent visitor from Guayaquil, and Stuart and John Clark were close by. All of the evangelical missionaries passing through were pressed into service.

Right from the start Clarence imposed a standard of absolute excellence for all HCJB productions, no matter how spontaneous or unrehearsed. From the initial half-hour daily broadcast, they gradually increased the Spanish programming time, then added English, and almost from the start, Quichua as well. HCJB's first convert, Señora Carmela De Ochoa, who phoned in that first week to say she wanted to know more about the living Christ, was fluent in Quichua. "I learned it from the servants in our home, and now I can preach the gospel to them," she said.

"Señora Ochoa's conversion so early in our broadcasting assured us that we were not on a wild goose chase. Even if there were only thirteen receivers, people were listening, and coming to Christ. And with daily broadcasting, sales of radios soared, multiplying our audience," C. W. reported.

In their initial presentation to the government, the founding group had stressed that the station would be first educational, second cultural, and then religious. Clarence adhered to this policy relentlessly, making sure there was no back-to-back religious programming.

For their educational segment, they developed "The University of the Air." After preparing programs of agricultural helps for the Indians, for instance, they'd go to the University: "Will you put these programs under your name?" The University was delighted to do so. Carlos Andrade Marín, the very helpful secretary to the President who had been a university student at that time, prepared health and hygiene programs. Francisco Cruz, a university professor, came to Jones: "We'll do anything we can to help you." Thus Cruz began broadcasting for HCJB, eventually becoming station manager. At that time, Cruz was not an evangelical, but he was a patriot. "These men accepted HCJB—the foreigner and evangelical—simply because we were benefiting their country," Jones and Larson felt sure.

From the start, most of HCJB's music was live, a feature that has kept HCJB in a class by itself. Clarence brought together the HCJB Ecuadorian Orchestra, one of the first groups to have their native songs written down and arranged for them. A classical string trio performed, and Clarence trained a fine Spanish singing group.

Especially in the very early days, the Jones family had to provide a good deal of the music: Clarence on trombone and

Kath on organ. Kath did a classical music program on the wheezy old pump organ, with Marian learning to read music as she played the foot pedal part on the lowest notes of the keyboard, and little Pedro on his knees, pushing the pedals by hand when Kath got tired of pumping. Then Grace Larson brought in a novel organ that had a movable keyboard—you could shift it up or down to change the key. Kath was delighted because this did away with having to transpose music. The Three-J's sang often—Katherine, Marian; and Marjorie, and when Nancy came along it was the Four-J's. Clarence encouraged musically skilled missionaries like Muriel Moffat, a fine classical pianist and contralto soloist, and operatic soprano Helen Ledar to come up from the jungle as frequently as possible.

Whether Ecuadorian, Spanish, or Quichua, ethnic, classical, or gospel, HCJB's music was always bright and appealing. Katherine remembers the time she was assisting at a birth and the doctor was practically dancing around the bed to the music of HCJB!

Jones handled the News Service, laying down the policy of no commentary whatsoever. At first the newspapers were the only source for news. Then UPI and AP began to send coded signals over the radio. Now the teletype is used and clicks away around the clock.

Early in HCJB's programming, government officials approached Jones: "Since you keep English time," (Clarence presumed they meant exact, punctual time) "will you be time-keepers for Ecuador?" Clarence started with an old telegraph key, tapping out "da-da-da-DAAAA"—Morse code for "victory." (Now a Swiss chronometer tied into Washington gives an automatic signal.)

But it wasn't always easy "to keep English time." When C.W. told the new announcer to report at least half an hour before air time, "2:30 for sure," the young Spaniard turned up all smiles at 5:00 P.M. What was Jones to do? He couldn't fire the only trained announcer in the city. So with his limited Spanish, C. W. could only try again to explain that when "we at HCJB say 2:30, we mean it to the second. In fact, if you are not fifteen minutes early, you're late!"

Whatever they did at HCJB, it was done with flair. Although in those early days of radio there were no rules for how to put on a program, Clarence had learned a few tricks during his eight years of broadcasting in Chicago, and brought to HCJB the same creative energy that had provided such fun for Rader's young radio staff when Jones was in charge there. Clarence's "Spanish Galleon" program, telling Ecuador's history through tales of pirates and plunder, had Kath and the kids rattling chains across the studio floor, banging doors and closing treasure chests to create all sorts of sound effects. "Morning in the Mountains" for Spanish audiences, and "Ecuadorian Echoes" for evening English listeners, had a gripping allure. The "Mail Bag" brought greetings from the missionaries to the folks back home, while yet another program kept chidren at Quito's Alliance Academy in touch with their missionary parents in the jungles of Ecuador, Peru, and Colombia. Ruby Eicher Huston, Christian Eicher's daughter who had become a missionary mother in Colombia, recalled that "the joy of those broadcasts, and especially the one from the children, lifted our hearts many times."

Top left: An autographed photo of Richard W. Oliver, Clarence's
closest boyhood friend. It reads, "For Clarence Jones, my
own dear brother in the Lord, with much love. Richard W.
Oliver, December 15, 1918. Proverbs 27:9."

Top right: Paul Rader, founder of the Chicago Gospel Tabernacle.

Bottom: A Bible study group taught at Paul Rader's Tabernacle by
Clarence Jones. The Chicago Gospel Tabernacle, located at Clark,
Halsted, and Barry Sts., seated 5000 people, featured a concert
band of fifty musicians and a choir of 300. Every Sunday there
was scheduled a fourteen-hour radio broadcast, as well as an
hour-long daily CBS network program. This was where C.W.
picked up eight years of radio training.

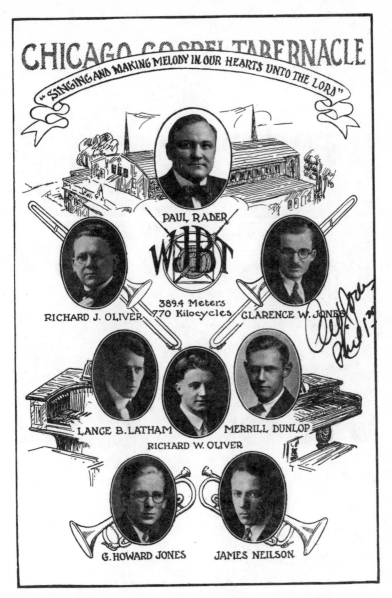

Frontispiece from "Gospel Songs of the Air"—a compilation
of songs written by members of the music staff of Chicago
Gospel Tabernacle and featured on Paul Rader's "Cathedral of
the Air" broadcast on radio station WJBT, Chicago.

Newlyweds Clarence and Katherine in Lima, Ohio, outside
the Welty residence.

Monday, Jan. 9, 1928

"Mi Valentino Mejor" 2/14/28
To Katherine.

Just a few threads of gold, woven,
perhaps, crudely into the fabric of that,
but nevertheless, with hands and heart
that love.

Absence and distance form a golden altar
Where my love for you is being refined:
Each languishing day is another fagot
Added to the flames,
And each longing mem'ry and wish is a
Breath, fanning the flames.
May God fashion some chalice of
Infinite design
From this unworthy heart of mine,
To convey to you in language more
expressively beautiful than earthly words —
And more lasting than symbols of time —
The story of my love for you —
Holding, the while, my soul's eternal devotion.

A page from C.W.'s diary: a valentine to Katherine. Written
February 14, 1928, while aboard ship, bound for Venezuela.

Left: Clarence Jones, daughter Marian, and Katherine. In Lake
   Harbor, Michigan, in 1920, just before their trip to
   Philadelphia.
Right: The Clarence Jones family, in 1927: Katherine and
   C.W. with Marjorie and Marian. This photo appeared in
   their first prayer letter.

Left: C.W. with son Dick, fourteen months old.
Right: The Jones family.

Top left: Clarence and Katherine Jones.
Top right: Dick Jones.
Bottom: Clarence Jones and Katherine explaining the work of HCJB.

Top: Guayaquil, Ecuador. The Guayas River is in background.
Bottom: Ambato, Ecuador.

The cover of a promotional booklet inaugurating the 10,000-watt shortwave transmitter financed by LeTourneau.

The Radio Rodante, a gospel sound truck, in the 1940s in the city of Otavalo.

Top: HCJB's first transmitter, which boasted 250 watts of
  broadcast power.
Bottom: TV antenna atop Mt. Pichincha overlooking Quito.

Top: Photo taken in 1955. From left to right: C.W. Jones, Reuben Larson, and D.S. Clark.

Bottom: The Founding Fathers, 1971. From left to right: Grace Larson, Reuben Larson, Paul Young, Clarence Jones, Katherine Jones, Ruth Clark, J.D. Clark, Erma Clark, D.S. Clark. In Quito.

Work of any kind
is acceptable.
There is no high work
or low work—
only a job to be done.
C. W. Jones

16

With all this involvement, quite naturally life in the Jones
household had to revolve around radio. The day started early,
with the news at 7:00 A.M., followed by "Morning in the
Mountains." Somewhere between the two the family tried to
squeeze in breakfast together, usually about 7:15. Clarence was
often tied up for breakfast, working in the studio, so while the
children ate, Kath would teach them a verse for the day.

They also had to make their beds and hang up their pajamas
before setting off for school on horseback. (If they didn't, they
could expect a swat from Father when they got home, but never
a slap across the face.) At the evening meal they tried having
family devotions, but the rules were never hard and fast. Again,
if Daddy had to be in the studio, they would carry on without
him, reading *The Daily Light* and joining hands around the table
while the children took turns praying.

Jones was not rigid about his own devotions. "I know that
practicing an early watch is a good discipline," Jones concedes.
"But I learned to worship God anyplace, anytime, walking along
the trail or up the mountain. You have to be able to be flexible
when radio is your life—sometimes you're up all night."

Clarence did try to set aside time every day to spend reading
and praying with Katherine. He didn't share all the problems of

the mission with her. "As a board, we decided that some things don't get shared, even with Kath. Some burdens you bear alone—the fewer who know, the better. Other things I simply did not want to burden her with."

But the pace was an impossible one. For the first months, HCJB was virtually a one-man operation. Eric had opened a station in Guayaquil. Clarence's brother Howard and wife Lillian came down but only briefly because Lillian's fair skin could not tolerate the strong equatorial sun. The Clarks, Reuben Larson, and Paul Young gave themselves freely, but they all had regular assigned jobs to do with their mission.

Most meetings for HCJB business had to be at 10 or 11 P.M., sometimes even midnight or as late as 1 A.M. This left Clarence managing the station, liaising with the government, preparing and scheduling programs, and practicing music with the singers and orchestra. Clarence found it hard not to expect from amateurs the same standard of performance he'd been used to with the professional Chicago staff. He had to fight against trying to impose Chicago "I-want-it-yesterday" time in the land of mañana.

In addition to the station work, at every opportunity, C. W. was out peddling radios, not only to increase the listening audience, but to "put something in the pantry" because funds were slow coming.

There were still times when Clarence was almost overcome with feelings of longing for his old friend Richard Oliver, with a sense of sadness and incompleteness in starting the station without Oliver's help. Kath would comfort him: "The Lord is absolutely sufficient to bring you through."

Katherine was doing her best to be hostess to the government people constantly coming and going through the busy household. The missionaries often stayed weeks and months at a time. She had help from Felipe, the gardener "who came with the house," and son Pedro, who served as "houseboy," and an Ecuadorian nanny for baby Dick. Kath was also pregnant again. They were having all sorts of technical problems too. Often Clarence and Katherine were winding transformers at midnight.

"We didn't understand what we were doing, but somehow we got it right." Then Clarence decided they needed to augment the power coming into the transmitter so they could beam the signal even farther over the mountains. A fine Ecuadorian engineer designed the needed equipment, but would not build it. As a Catholic, he felt he had to be antagonistic to this Protestant work. (Now he is a good friend.) That left Clarence working alone until two or three in the morning, night after night, trying to crank more power out of their little transmitter.

Finally, Katherine had had enough. "You don't need a family," she announced at the dinner table one night. "I might as well leave and take the children back to the States!"

There was a stunned silence. The conversation that followed became so serious that Kath and Clare went into the bedroom to discuss it further. Marian and Marjorie were terrified. They adored their father. Mommy really wouldn't take them away. Or would she?

They tried to listen at the door, but the walls were two feet thick. Marian went outside, climbed up the ivy, and hid under the casement window. It was very quiet, so she sneaked a peek. To Marian's astonishment, Kath and Clare were down on their knees praying.

With that matter straightened away, Kath took Clarence "for a long walk in the garden."

"As well as it not being right for you to spend so little time with the family, I really can't take much more of your moodiness," she told him. Clare was taken totally by surprise. He had no idea he'd been behaving that way. "He was never moody after that," Kath says. "Consistently throughout his life, Clarence has chosen to allow the Lord to change him."

Right from the beginning there were financial problems. "We started with a promise—Jeremiah 33:3, " Jones would say. And that was about all they had, a promise. With the deepening depression in the States, many dear friends who had had every intention of supporting the Joneses simply could not keep up their commitments. Try as Rader would, he could not keep the money coming. "The Tabernacle members got tired of

Paul's plugging for funds for the Joneses every Sunday," Rader's sister recalled.

Less than $1000 in all came in during that first year, 1932, and made up their entire mission budget. The Joneses lived from hand to mouth, never knowing where the next nickel was coming from. (The children wore several layers of cardboard in their shoes to keep out the Quito dampness, and thought that was what everyone did. Katherine and Clarence never let them feel poor.)

With Felipe's help, the Joneses put in a big garden. Felipe would only plant "at the right time of the moon," but one day, C. W. insisted they "skip that nonsense and plant corn." Felipe shrugged and put it in—but no corn came up. After that, they left Felipe to his own way, and enjoyed wonderful crops. Katherine learned to make all sorts of concoctions using the cheapest foods available, so that there was always something to feed the steady stream of visitors. And somehow, Katherine managed to have extra jars of pickles and jams to send to sick friends.

Clarence hustled. In addition to selling radios, one day the same young secretary from the president's office, Carlos Andrade Marín, who was now principal of Academia Mejía, the largest boys' school in Ecuador, came to Clarence: "Would you give classes in English? And we want you to teach by the West Point method." What he meant was personal discipline, punctuality, and honesty, with no cheating on exams.

Teaching for two or three hours daily, Jones started with fifty high schoolers and ended up with 150 in his class; these were all high-family Ecuadorians who would go on into government and professional positions. Some students sat on chairs, others stood at the back, taking notes as best they could. It was all by rote. Since they didn't have textbooks, C. W. mimeographed sheets as they went along, and in accordance with an initial agreement with Andrade Marín, every third line included a quotation from the Bible, usually something from the Psalms or Proverbs, and Jones took the opportunity to explain what the

Bible meant. In Latin America there is a special relationship between the teacher and pupil, with great respect for the teacher, and Clarence counted those years as some of the most exacting, the most trying and difficult, but the most fruitful years of all his ministry in Ecuador.

Then Clarence was asked to direct the Quito Municipal Band. Clarence had noticed that as the band marched down the street, they didn't use their drum. For a former Salvation Army man, this was unthinkable. So he asked them, "Why don't you fellows have your bass drum or your snare drum going?" To which they haughtily replied, "Only a circus band does that!" Well, Clarence never did try to change cultural mores, but he did his best with those worn-out, dilapidated instruments, working with the nationals, bringing them to a proficiency they never had dreamed of. They performed every Sunday afternoon in the El Ejido Plaza and broadcast one night each week from the lawn at Quinto Cornston. "Work of any kind is acceptable," Clarence insisted. "There is no high work or low work; only a job to be done."

Correspondence with Eric Williams in Guayaquil reveals the struggles both men were going through to keep the radio stations functioning properly, to overcome family illnesses, and to keep bread and butter on the table. Yet there was a good deal of banter and lighthearted repartee: "So there is thieving in the post office," Williams wrote. "Well, old man, since we never get any money, it doesn't matter to us!" And another time: "Still burning gasoline? I never knew a man with as much nervous energy as you, Clare. Wish you were here to fire me up and get me going again." Eric was selling radio equipment and doing repairs; he and Clarence were talking about starting a Radio News Magazine: "Anything to make money; we must do something if we are to exist!"

In May 1933, after a number of checks bounced, the bank holding all Worldwide Christian Courier funds folded. (The Chicago Gospel Tabernacle eventually went bankrupt.) This left the Joneses and the Williamses absolutely strapped. An electric bill for $6.15 came in, and Clarence just could not find the money. There was nothing else to do—they would have to go off the air.

That was the day Clarence went to the bottom of the garden, taking a chair with him to the little toolshed. "Dear God, are we finding out now that we've made a terrible mistake? Are we to carry on with HCJB, or pack it in and go home?" Clarence spent the whole day waiting before the Lord, without food or any interruptions. "This was a low spot, a valley in my life, and in the history of the mission," C.W. recalls vividly. "There wasn't any human hope at that time, but *there was something in my heart that looked to the Lord to do something.*"

To support
a God-ordered project
He always has
God-ordered donors.
C. W. Jones

That darkest day became the greatest day for Clarence Jones as God met him and lifted his spirits, giving him joy even in the darkness, granting him confidence that HCJB would go on.

"The Lord made it plain to me that Jeremiah 33:3 was still good: 'Call unto *me*', he said, 'not to a church or people who cannot follow through. *I will answer. I'll show you great and mighty things—bigger than you've ever dreamed of, Clarence.'* This very positive message came to me so clearly.

"I was thinking too that day about the plush studios we had left in Chicago. I had trusted God to do 'great things,' to give us the best. And all he'd given us was an old microphone in a rough packing case, and this mud-walled sheepshed. Then I heard that still small voice: 'Whom do you broadcast about?' and I answered, 'Why, Jesus Christ, the Son of God, the Lamb of God.' And the Spirit whispered: 'Can you think of a better place to talk about the Lamb of God than from a sheepshed?' And of course I couldn't."

God reassured Clarence that *doubts will come to everyone to help him find out if he's in the right place. "Without a real conscientious doubt, you have no place for overcoming fear; and in spite of what you see, God will do something for you. God teaches lessons through the negative as well as the positive."*

Clare went back to do the evening broadcast with fresh fervor, with renewed vigor and inspiration. Katherine, who had grown up quoting *Prayer* by Reinhold Niebuhr, "God grant me serenity to accept the things I cannot change...," courageously agreed to try again.

"There are never mountain tops without valleys in between," said Clarence as he set his sights on the next peak. Now he was joyfully, unshakably confident that somehow God was going to do "a new thing," to make a way where there was no way, absolutely assured that HCJB was in Quito not only to stay, but to grow from "this little acorn," as he referred to the 250-watt transmitter, into a mighty, giant oak of undreamed proportions.

Stuart Clark came by. "Something's been bothering you for the last few days," he said. And Clarence told him the whole story. Ultimately D. S. was able to advance the needed funds. (This was not the first nor the last time D. S. or J. D. came to the Joneses financial rescue.)

Praising the Lord, Clarence went to the bank and arranged a mortgage to cover the next lot of bills. "Climbing is not always going forward; sometimes you go sideways, looking for a better way to climb the mountain," Jones insisted. Then he fired off a powerful flyer, highlighted with a stirring poem, "The Call of the Andes."

Where blue skies are swelling
The Andes are telling
Of dark shadows dwelling—
  So long;
Where darkness is falling
Sad hearts there are calling
With sorrows enthralling
  Too long.
But now o'er the Andes there comes beaming
The Gospel of Life, brightly gleaming
And still, where sin is betraying
And burdens are weighing
The Andes are saying—
  "How long?"

Jones laid out the entire situation:
—*We have had to mortgage our transmitter, the heart of our work.*
—*We need $5000 to purchase this property.*
—*We believe that God has inspired and will prosper HCJB— four letters that mean South America's greatest chance to hear the gospel in this generation.*

He included testimonies from Ecuador, Columbia, and Peru of lives blessed through "hearing the gospel in this new way"— breaking down the problem, translating the need into understandable, "everybody-do-a-little" terms.

It worked. There were still difficult months financially, but that valley was pretty well behind them.

With the number of receivers in the country multiplying rapidly, radio HCJB was cutting across every level of society, breaking down barriers to the gospel. Missionaries (many who had in fact strongly opposed the idea of Christian radio) were finding that where previously they were persecuted and stoned on the streets, now they could minister openly. And even when they encountered a "Protestants Not Welcome" sign on a door, inside they could hear *La Voz de los Andes*, HCJB. Everyone seemed to be listening.

From the start, Jones treated with great respect the privilege of broadcasting in a foreign culture. "We decided on a very simple policy," Jones explains. "*Never meddle in politics, and preach a positive gospel.*"

"We weren't there to shove a new religion down their throats, but simply to share the revelation of God: that Christ Jesus came into this world, being born of the virgin, lived a perfect life, and then went to the cross where by his shed blood he paid for the sins of men who would believe on him; that now he is at the right hand of the Father and he has sent his people out to tell this plain, wonderful story that God so loved the world that he gave his only begotten Son.

"That's essential, that's basic, that's final," Jones insists. "Nothing can be added to it, nothing need be subtracted from it. It's spiritually sound; it's the dynamic—the power of God unto salvation, the message that in its simplicity and purity, with the power of the Holy Spirit, can bring about transformation in the lives of university professors or Indian peasants. It's the everlasting message of God to sinful men in a dying world. It's the only hope. It's absolutely necessary and sufficient, and we thanked God for the privilege of proclaiming it."

At HCJB, Spanish programming always took top priority. Ecuadorians were hired and trained—announcers, technicians, engineers; and although C. W. would never give an advance on pay, a practice that was quite common in Latin America, he always paid in full and on time, and this integrity was appreciated. "These people weren't 'born-again evangelicals' to begin with," Jones admits. "Right from the start, we had a mission within a mission."

When some of this trained personnel moved over to staff other radio stations as they came into operation within the country, Jones too was right there, lending whatever expertise he could.

Jones set a standard that HCJB would not be an isolated missionary compound, but they would be useful members of the community. Thus he was delighted to teach school and lead the municipal band. During the Joneses' second Christmas in Quito, in spite of their own financial difficulties, through radio programs C. W. collected money and goods to make up baskets for the poor.

Jones encouraged the government to make use of the 20 percent broadcasting time over local frequencies agreed upon in their contract, and often the president was in their studio speaking to the people. An HCJB microphone stood on the podium during sessions of Congress. All the national holidays were recognized with great flourish, and as well, representatives from other embassies came out to share their special days with HCJB listeners, bringing singers and musicians; often the children too would come along for tea. Katherine had a constant procession of "top brass" through her home. Ruth and Erma Clark pitched in, helping to bake cakes and cookies, pouring coffee from the silver service which Kath's sister Ruth had sent down, and very helpfully serving as interpreters for Kath until she became fluent in Spanish.

The "Radio Rodante," or Traveling Radio, was frequently loaned for government use—a gospel sound truck, with public address system and radio hookup with Quito. Jones had gotten the idea from the highly successful "Box-Car Evangelism" of 1933 when he and Stuart Clark had been invited to take along HCJB's equipment on the government's "Silver Anniversary Exposition Train" celebrating twenty-five years of operating the Guayaquil-Quito railway. To link the isolated mountain capital with the seaport and coastal people had been a tremendous accomplishment, and all of Ecuador was in a mood to celebrate its success.

The little black-and-gold wood-burning locomotive, pulling its train of freshly painted exhibition cars strung with bright banners, puffed its way across the flatlands, chugging slowly up the tortuous canyons of the roaring Chan-Chan River, easing over the austere Andean heights, and stopping at every little settlement along this twisting thread of steel.

Most of the way, Clarence rode on the roof of the boxcar, shooting film with his movie camera. As the train slowed to a stop, he'd scamper down inside the HCJB special. At top 50-watt volume, the national anthem blared from the loudspeaker mounted on the boxcar, and the villagers ran with mouths gaping wide in wonder. Trains they had seen, but a singing boxcar! Never! Then D. S. would open the boxcar door; at the microphone, Clarence with his trombone would swing into a national hymn and military march.

The minister of Agriculture and Commerce would then step to the HCJB mike: "We are here to do honor to the intrepid vision and courage..." he would begin, but the crowd would shout him down. "Music, we want more music." So C. W. would sit down at the little portable organ and play some of the plaintive Ecuadorian melodies. From across the plain, from up and down the mountain the people were drawn by this new thing of a song floating loud and clear across the air.

"But they must come in and tour the coaches," the Minister pled. "Stop the music."

"Mr. Minister, you brought us along because you wanted powerful music to attract the crowds," D. S. graciously reminded. "You also said we could preach the gospel at each stop. So after this song I will preach and then the people will tour the train."

With the promise of more music after viewing the exposition, the crowd swooped through the train; C. W. played some more ("They were delighted with what C. W. could do with that trombone," D. S. recalls), and then the little train puffed its way to the next stop.

By mid-1934, Grace Larson's health had steadily failed following the birth and soon death of a child at Quinta Cornston. She stayed on with Kath for some months, then finally they headed home for medical treatment and a furlough that lasted two and one-half years. Clarence kept an eye on things at Dos Ríos for Reuben, providing supplies as required—"Please send out three mules and two horses with good saddles"—and visiting seven or eight times a year.

On one of the return trips, they'd risen at 4 A.M. in the dark and started along the narrow mule trail gouged out of the mountain side. It had been raining and the trail was slippery. C. W. was bringing up the rear when his horse stumbled and slid off the edge, falling straight down toward the bottom of the 1000-foot canyon. Suddenly they caught on a protruding tree and hung there on a little ledge, about 100 feet below the trail, with the horse lying across Jones's left leg.

Jones hollered, but no one answered. "As I lay there in the dark, I really thought this was the end," he recalls with some grimness. Finally the party realized that Jones was not following, and came back to search.

Dawn was just beginning to creep around the mountains as they heard his cry. "Are you there? Can we help you?" they called. "Yes. Come on down and get this horse off me!"

Skillfully the muleteers let themselves down; one took the horse by the head, the other by the tail and somehow got the brute on its feet and back onto the trail. They helped C. W. up, then they all remounted and rode off for Quito. There, as always, Clarence got a rousing welcome from his family, and the menagerie: the cross old parrot which they kept chained (or else he would nip the back of guests' legs), the handsome cats which chased the mice, the pet monkey Grace Larson had left with them, the numerous thoroughbred German shepherd guard dogs which Jones bred, and Marian's tiny white poodle, "Rags." ("To think I could fall in love with a little poodle," C. W., a "big dog" man, would say.)

"Clare could do anything with the animals," Kath recalls. When the monkey was determined to perch on top of the house, only C. W. could call him down. Each morning when Clarence looked out their bedroom window (where often they could see six mountain peaks, including the perfect cone of Cotopaxi, the world's highest active volcano), the monkey would be sitting on top of the little house Felipe had built for him on a pole by Kath and Clare's room, cocking his head from side to side, eyeing C. W. delightedly. Clarence and Marjorie fed and cared for all the animals.

With Father home, once more the fun would begin. "Daddy made things happen," the children remember. At noon and after work, he'd join the nationals for a rousing game of volleyball or soccer. Often there were picnics and barbecues. "Let's have a party," he'd say, and the missionaries and members of the American colony were always happy to come out to Quinta Cornston. Sometimes the municipal band would entertain on the front lawn. C. W. would organize sack races and three-legged races. Sitting down to eat, he'd be flipping water off his spoon onto some unsuspecting youngster.

"The little folks loved him, the babies, the preschoolers—he could talk to them all. And he had an unusual rapport with teenagers." His puns and jokes were always very clever and timely. "Wherever Father was, it was a party!" the children agree.

Yet sometimes they chafed under his strict discipline. Other children knew C. W. as the strictest of all the missionaries. The Joneses' children noticed that young visitors "could get away with almost anything," but with his own, C. W. would be very severe, very demanding. They had distinguished dinner guests so often, from the American colony or the Ecuadorian government, and high-ranking visitors to the country, and Jones would never tolerate his children speaking out of turn, or poor manners of any kind. "He expected instant obedience with only an interchange of glances," Marjorie remembers.

Punishment would be with the belt, or a cuff across the ear, or a child would be sent to bed with bread and water for the next meal. The worst punishment Marian remembers was having to wear overalls for two weeks, and she was absolutely mortified when her school-girl crush, the handsome Galo Plaza (the future president and ambassador to the United Nations), came to Quinta Cornston and saw her dressed like that.

"Daddy definitely did not count to ten before he punished us," Marian recalls, "but it was never unjust. Sometimes he would be fiercely angry and frustrated. We wouldn't know why. We were afraid of this."

Still, for all his severity and strictness, for all the demands he made on his family, there was no other place they would rather be, "because he was an example of all he expected," his children say simply. They loved him, even worshipped him for his total committment, his total dedication, for the work he was doing, and his ability and excellence in all that he did. "We knew there was no other man in the world like our Dad." They each felt honored to be his child. They were "terribly proud of him. But that was to be a family secret. We were not to boast of his accomplishments to others. Our Dad was so special that we didn't have to broadcast it—others knew it too."

And, ye fathers,
provoke not your children
to wrath:
but bring them up
in the nurture
and admonition
of the Lord.
Ephesians 6:4

18

Clarence always taught that "marital disharmony equals family disaster," and the children never recall being exposed to any arguing between their parents. Clarence maintained that "love is a fragile flower needing cultivating if it is to grow"; that "father-mother relations are foundational to a happy family circle and thus father must continue to be a full-orbed husband to his wife for their children's sake." Consequently the children often saw him saying "I love you" to Kath, accompanied by a box of Whitman Sampler chocolates, a rare treasure in Quito in those days. Their memories are of a "very tender, thoughtful husband who treated Kath like a queen." But then, Kath always acted the part, always the lady wearing pretty dresses and being the gracious hostess.

Best of all were the meal times when they were "just family." "Daddy was interested in each one of us, wanting to know what we were doing and thinking." At home they received the *Reader's Digest* and *National Geographic* as well as the *Book of the Month*, and there was always lively discussion over current books and articles.

There were treasured outings riding horseback through the fragrant eucalyptus woods, or roaring over the mountain roads on the motorcycle with Kath and the three children tucked in the sidecar to picnic on the rocks by a rushing stream.

"Mother was always available to us, and we turned to her instinctively and unceasingly in our need. But our time with Daddy was so limited that we cherished it. We knew he was a very busy man, yet the time he spent with his family was always 'quality' time."

What they looked forward to most was their annual holiday at the ocean. (C. W. never could tolerate these missionaries who "boast they have worked twenty-five years without a vacation." He knew how to work, but he also knew how to play.)

Kath would shop for three weeks' supplies, then pack up the children, and in the dark at 6 A.M., board the train for Guayaquil, usually taking along Pedro to help out. John Reed loaned them his fisherman's retreat—a split-bamboo hut on stilts with thatch grass roof, set in an idyllic tropical paradise on the Isle of Puña at the mouth of the Guayas River.

For the first three days, Clarence slept; then for three days he read. By that time, the children would have finished exploring the island, C. W. would be rejuvenated, and he gave himself totally to the family in "marvelous, glorious, imaginative play."

They hiked along the white sand beaches and swam in the quiet coves, or frolicked in the great breakers. They flew kites and played softball when the tide was out. They made magnificent sandcastles and sand boats with three spools up front, two behind, and a sail to race along the hard sand. They picnicked on the shore, then together experienced the soul-filling beauty of sunsets where the whole South Pacific sky was a wash of oranges, reds, and pinks.

At night the children slept on the porch under the stars, so close they could reach up and pick them out of the sky, shivering as the lunar high tides rushed right under their little cottage. Sometimes Clarence would waken them, "Let's go fishing." Taking a flashlight and poles with a nail on the end, they'd walk along the beach, and in the little pools left by the receding tide, they would spear blue crabs for a delicious midnight feast.

In Quito, the staff almost dreaded C. W.'s return from

vacation. He'd come back bursting with new projects, new ideas that would have them all jumping.

Kath's role continued to be a varied one, combining the duties of mother and wife, one who was always anticipating Clare's needs and providing for them, managing a "Grand Central Station" household, arranging and practicing music, and writing and producing radio shows. Tardiness has always been a problem for Kath; somehow she managed to be on time for broadcasts, but barely so, much to C. W.'s chagrin. "Daddy would get so impatient—he lived by a clock; and Mother was always late. She constantly drove Daddy right up the wall," the children confided.

Floods and revolutions compounded the problems of house-keeping in Quito at that time. One severe rainstorm swept a sea of mud through the Quinta. For the revolutions, Katherine always had to have extra food put away because the big American flag on the door gave immunity to all who sought shelter. So the neighbors would crowd in, overflowing the studios, the living room, and dining room. During the shelling, they took shelter in the low crawl space under the house.

"I shall always treasure the memory of Daddy's strength and security during revolutions," Marjorie recalls. At one point, an armored car pulled up at the gate. C. W went out. "We'd like to listen on your radio to see which side is winning!" they requested. So although all broadcasting was shut down, while Kath served the soldiers cake and coffee, C. W. made radio contact. They chatted awhile, then most cordially went back to their war. At 7 P.M. every evening, the revolution was called off and C. W. could go about the business of the station. At sunup, the revolution was on again.

Katherine discovered that some nationals expected that a white person should be able to do anything, so when the cook's wife was having a baby, they took it for granted Kath would handle the delivery. When the time came, Kath staunchly went off to the little hut where she got a basin of water boiling over the little one-burner *fagon*, then, discovering there was nothing to wrap the baby in, rushed back for one of Clarence's white shirts. Suddenly the baby was coming, and Katherine got terrified. She phoned Dr. Andrade Marín, who had become their family doctor, "I'm delivering a baby and I don't know what to do!"

Kath tied the cord in three places, just to be sure; Andrade Marín arrived and told her, "You've done just fine!" Then he cut the cord and tied it properly. "It's one thing to have a baby and quite another to deliver one," Kath protested.

Katherine's own Nancy had arrived by this time. Again it was a difficult pregnancy, with Kath having an infection which could not be treated until after delivery. Kath was totally drained emotionally and physically, but a few weeks at the coast with baby Nancy and a wet nurse brought back the sparkle and bounce.

And then Nancy contracted whooping cough which developed into double pneumonia. They set up a round-the-clock vigil by her cot, keeping a stove going through the night for hot water because when she would start to turn blue, they quickly had to plunge the tiny form into first a hot, then a cold bath. J. D. and Ruth, D. S. and Erma all took turns. For several days and nights, the Clarks were so busy, they never had time to change clothes.

One day when Nancy seemed to be a little better, ten-year-old Marian was left to watch. Clare was in the front hall waiting for the engineer who was to drive him out to Ambato on radio business. Suddenly God spoke to him: "Go in to the baby."

Clare rushed in. Nancy had turned blue and had stopped breathing. Gathering her in his arms, Clare called to Kath, "Phone Andrade Marín!"

"She's dead and it's my fault," a heartbroken Marian wailed.

"No, my little one, God will look after her," Clarence said consolingly.

The doctor was playing in a championship tennis match two blocks away. He left the court and dashed over, plunged a needle directly into Nancy's heart, and miraculously life returned to the tiny body. Again C. W. thanked God for "Divine

Radar"—the Lord's unmistakable guidance that had called him back into the baby's room.

Whether the Jones family was simply accident-prone, or whether they were being stalked by the Adversary, they seemed to have more than their share of tragedies and near-tragedies. Each day when Marian and Marjorie went off to school on their ponies, as soon as they were out of sight, Marian took off in a gallop and Marjorie would stand on the horse's back doing circus tricks. One day the horse threw Marian, dragging her along the ground for some distance. Miraculously there were no serious injuries, but Marjorie spilled the beans and after that the two girls walked the mile-and-a-half to the Alliance Academy.

Another day, while riding downtown with Clarence in the back of the Radio Rodante, the bigger girls were supposed to be minding little Nancy. But this "slippery eel" escaped their grasp and when C. W. had to stop suddenly, Nancy smashed her head against a piece of the equipment, opening a nasty gash and bringing on a concussion.

On another occasion, Marian fell from quite a height out of the big oak tree in the garden. Once, when the two girls were playing on the swing that hung from its branches, for some reason the two German shepherds became excited and attacked the girls. In the studio Clarence heard their screams and dashed out, grabbing a cane from the front hall when he saw what was happening, and managed to beat off the dogs. The girls and Clarence still carry scars from that dreadful fight.

But ye shall receive power,
after that the Holy Ghost
is come upon you:
and ye shall be witnesses
unto me both in Jerusalem,
and in all Judaea,
and in Samaria,
and unto the uttermost part
of the earth.
Acts 1:8

As the years ticked by, Kath was beginning to think she would never again see her father, or for that matter, America. Then Reuben and Grace returned to Quito in early January 1937, and Reuben was loaned by the Alliance to HCJB and a ministry of evangelism-at-large throughout Ecuador. The Joneses could now begin to make plans for a furlough.

In addition to the Larsons being back in Ecuador, an outstanding member had been added to the HCJB staff—the very distinguished Manuel Garrido Aldama, a Spanish priest who had been wonderfully converted in London, England, and from there had gone on to Peru with the Evangelical Union of South America. "We must have Aldama," John Clark had recommended after a visit to Peru.

At first, Aldama could not see how "the gospel preached by radio could have lasting results. I thought it had to be by personal contact," Aldama recounts. "When I heard that some American missionary was trying to establish a radio station in Quito to preach the gospel to the Spanish-speaking people, my reaction was scornful: 'These Americans will try anything that is new and out of the ordinary, even in preaching the gospel.' "

But then Aldama met Clyde Taylor, a coworker who was placing a radio at the entrance of his church, and with the music of the Voice of the Andes was attracting passers-by into the service. Clarence, too, went after Aldama, keeping his daughter Olga in the Jones home while the Aldamas went to England for a few months to discuss the whole new concept with their mission board.

Gradually Aldama caught the vision, and became a powerful radio preacher. With his beautiful Spanish, his deep understanding of the Roman religion and Latin culture, very quickly Aldama's fifteen-minute breakfast hour, "Luz Cotidiana" (Daily Light) was drawing the largest listener response. Other Spanish ministries were added. "We stay home from the movies to hear what Aldama has to say," people wrote in.

On the whole, the radio work at HCJB was proceeding nicely. The sale of receivers was booming, and Clarence had been especially delighted when a priest came into the little downtown sales office they'd set up—the Quito Radio Agency. C. W. tuned in a set for him, opening up the volume. "No, no!" the priest protested. "I want a radio that speaks softly, so no one can hear me listening to *la Voz de los Andes.* All the other priests have radios, and they're listening too," he confided to Clarence.

The poorer people could not yet afford radios, so C. W. had placed fifty HCJB "Listening Posts" around Ecuador: *la cajita magica que canta!*—"the little magic box that sings." These sturdy receiving sets were entrusted to Christians who would share them with their friends—like the tailor with sixty-five neighbors jamming into his little home or the cotton mill worker who gathered all the children of the village into his *sala* for the "Escuela Dominical del Aire" (Sunday School of the Air).

Another miracle had occurred in the Ecuadorian Congress where, according to their statutes, all HCJB property, as was the case with any foreign-owned property, would revert to the country at the end of five years. Now it so happened that a special bill was up for a third reading, granting exemption from this statute to a certain foreign-owned, non-profit school.

The president stood up and addressed the Congress: "Gentlemen, I am standing before a microphone of HCJB. Through the courtesy of HCJB, all the citizens of Ecuador know what this government is doing. I would like to ask that the name of HCJB be added to the bill now before us." This passed without a dissenting vote.

As well as the 250-watt long wave for Quito and local broadcasting, a new 1000-watt transmitter was now reaching the 80-90 million Spanish-speaking people of South and Central America. Also, Clarence had bought himself a little 100-watt ham radio and by playing around with the antenna and by shifting bands, he was making two- or three-minute voice contact with other ham operators around the world. The vision began to grip him: At HCJB they were reaching their "Judea"—Ecuador, and their "Samaria"—Central and South America. *What would it take to broadcast the gospel via a strong, consistently clear signal "to the uttermost part of the earth"?*

It pays
not to listen
too long
nor to speak
too soon.
C. W. Jones

"No good thing will he withhold from them that walk right up and take it." Katherine Jones quoted Howard Ferrin's favorite Bible verse as she and C. W. lounged in exquisite comfort on the Scottish banana boat which carried only twelve passengers on its maiden voyage to San Pedro, the port city near Los Angeles.

"We have no supporters, so we may have to dig ditches," C. W. had written to his father-in-law, advising him of their furlough in early 1938.

Adam Welty was on the dock to meet them. "If the seven of us are going to get across the States, we must have a car," he decided, arranging with a friend to stand guarantor for a $300 bank loan.

And so, in a 1935 gray Ford, they set off along the West Coast. "Where are we going?" C. W. would ask. "Just keep driving—I'll tell you when we get there," Welty would answer. He'd be studying names on the mailboxes, and when he recognized a familiar German name, he'd instruct C. W. to pull over. And then Welty, supported by the German Mennonites in Ohio, would go in. Very soon, the lady of the house would come out, hug all six Joneses and take them in for the night.

People would ask the children, "What church are you?" Innocently, the children would answer, "We are Christian."

They had known no denominational barriers in all their youthful experience in Quito.

One happy stop was with Charles Fuller in Pasadena. Fuller had heard their 1000-watt station and had written to Quito: "I want you to be a missionary arm for my work. But I'll put my programs on the air only if you'll let me pay for the time." This had been a new concept for Jones. So he figured out the cost and cut it in half. The Old Fashioned Revival Hour sent down their seventeen-inch discs and in 1937 went on as HCJB's first "pay-as-you-use-it" plan, which now has been adopted for all sponsored programming. Up until then, all programs had been live.

At the Church of the Open Door in Los Angeles, the minister saw C. W. sitting in the congregation. "Clarence Jones—what are you doing here?" he demanded. "Come up and tell us about your work." Clarence had known all the great preachers from when they had ministered together at Rader's Tab in Chicago, and thus doors were opened as the Joneses made their way across the States.

Driving through the mountains near Pike's Peak, Colorado, they barely escaped serious injury when suddenly a car approached them at high speed head-on in their lane. There was no shoulder on their side of the road; but somehow, narrowly missing a large truck, Clarence managed to cross over to the other shoulder. The dirt was hard, so Clare was able to keep control of the car. "We all got out and held a Thanksgiving service," Jones recalls fervently.

Now, before Jones had left Quito, HCJB had received an offer from a radio technician in Chicago to sell them a used 5000-watt transmitter for $10,000. The trustees had authorized C. W. to have a look at it, and if he could find the money, to go ahead and purchase it. But Jones's year in the States was almost at an end, and all he had raised was $3000. Somewhat discouraged, they headed for Lima, Ohio, and a last visit with Kath's family before sailing from New York.

At the rescue mission, a telegram was waiting. "If you want to see me before sailing, come." Signed R. G. LeTourneau. LeTourneau had risen to international prominence through his innovative design of large, earth-moving equipment. One of God's choice businessmen, he gave at least 90 percent of earnings to missions, living quite modestly, at every opportunity sharing his testimony of God's faithfulness on tithing-plus.

"Let's go!" Clarence jumped, chartering a plane, and taking along his godly father-in-law "to do the praying."

LeTourneau listened to C. W.'s report noncommitally, looking out the window as Clarence spoke. Then he swung around in his chair, elbows on his desk, and said, "What I'd really like you to do is build a radio station in the Philippines. I'll underwrite the whole operation."

Clarence's mind whirled. The Philippines! Wasn't this what Turnbull had envisioned? A station in the Philippines for the vast hordes of the Pacific and the Orient, one in South America, and another in Israel. Jones too shared this vision to blanket the world with the gospel by radio. Was God beckoning them to broaden their *World* Radio Missionary Fellowship?

But the answer in his heart came back, "No. Stay with Ecuador." With an inward sigh, Clarence stood to his feet and put his papers back in his briefcase. "I'm sorry, Mr. LeTourneau. My call is to South America. We have a long way to go with that project. You'll have to find someone else for the Philippines," and he turned to walk out the door.

"I just may do that," R. G. replied. "But in the meantime," he said, looking up from his scribbling, "I want to help you get that 5000-watt transmitter." He handed Clarence a check for $7000— the exact amount lacking.

"We didn't need wings to fly into Chicago that night," Clarence remembers. The purchase papers for the used transmitter were all drawn up and Clarence took out his pen to sign. "But I couldn't. Something held my hand back from that piece of paper." The "Divine Radar" was flashing a red light. In confusion C. W. turned to the engineer. "I just don't feel free to go ahead with this. We'll be in touch."

Jones was bewildered. Here was the transmitter. He had the check and authorization to buy it. How could he explain his action to the other trustees?

Totally baffled, Clare joined the family for a final tour of New England, where they were entertained by two outstanding Christian women: Kathryn Evans, a dear friend of Richard Oliver and executive secretary of the New England Fellowship; and her sister Elizabeth, chairman of the Boston Business Women's Council.

"What a pleasure those children were to have in the house!" the sisters recalled warmly. "They were so well disciplined, and they adored Clarence Jones. He was a wonderful father."

Late one night, Jones had a phone call from a member of the new Home Advisory Council, John Meredith in Chicago. "C.W., about that used transmitter we're planning to buy—it's a heap of junk!" "That can't be," Jones responded immediately. "The Lord has provided the exact amount to purchase it, to the very dollar." And then he remembered the flashing red light. "Tell me more, John."

Meredith recounted how his nephew, Clarence Moore, a clever amateur radio technician, had heard Jones telling of HCJB over Moody radio, WMBI; then the Lord had impelled Moore to visit Meredith in Chicago, not knowing anything about the proposed transmitter. Along with another radio buff, Bill Hamilton, Moore had looked over the equipment with growing dismay. It was obsolete and they could see no way to rebuild it.

C. W. was taken aback. "This changes everything. I've got to talk to those young men." Moore and Hamilton flew all night, and amidst the carousing of New Year's Eve, 1938, the three men sat down in a Boston hotel.

"For a year I've been trying to raise money to buy a 5000-watt transmitter; God has sent the money in, but now you tell me it would be foolish to go ahead with the purchase of the only piece of equipment available, so far as I know, for this kind of money. What are we to do?" Jones turned to Moore with the same certainty that had stopped him from signing the purchase agreement. "Could you build us a new 5000-watt transmitter for $10,000?" Moore and Hamilton started to figure up component costs. Impossible. But as they prayed together, Moore knew it could be done, and that under God he would do it.

LeTourneau set aside a corner of his Peoria, Illinois, factory and Moore took a leave of absence from teaching high school and pastoring a Mennonite church. One day R. G. came by on the scooter he rode to get around his sprawling plant. "For very little more money, we could double the output to 10,000 watts," Moore told him. "Go ahead," LeTourneau ordered.

And so it was that instead of a used 5000-watt unit, in late 1939 Clarence Moore arrived in Quito with a brand new 10,000-watt transmitter, and he set about getting it operational.

We dare not go on awakening . . .
interest in the gospel . . .
unless somehow
we also can nourish
and preserve the results.
C. W. Jones

Clarence Jones now faced a real problem. He was the one who had outlined the radio and communication laws for Ecuador, and now he had to abide by them. This meant he could not have such a strong transmitter within the city limits. Several of the embassies had located close to Quinta Cornston, and by 1939 the area had become exclusively residential.

In Iñaquito, "little Quito," a suburb on the north side, Stuart Clark and C. W. found a choice property, a cabbage patch actually, larger than HCJB anticipated for their need; but fortunately the Alliance too was looking for a new school site, so together they bought up the entire large city block.

The transmitter house was first to go up, then the guest home. C. W. supervised the burnt-brick construction: trenching the foundations, then piling in pyramids of stones which were cemented together. (This saved cement.) Square corners seemed to be a new idea to many of his crew, but C. W. brought out his rule and plumb line and got them straightened up. "When you get to the top of the door opening, put across a big wooden beam," he instructed. He taught them carpentry, "but with the green eucalyptus, you could hang a door and in six months you'd be able to drive a horse through the cracks that had opened," C. W. says.

For the guest house, which would also be their home, Katherine selected a center-hall floor plan from *Good Housekeeping* magazine, complete with washroom on the main floor, and a nicely laid out, built-in kitchen. Instead of a garage, the studio and control room went in to the right of the front door.

"Clare would tackle anything and do it well!" Katherine enthuses. Well, almost anything. There was the fieldstone fireplace which Clare built back-to-back with another fireplace in the main floor bedroom. But he forgot to put in two flues, so when he tried to light a fire in both rooms, one would go out. Very quickly the bedroom fireplace was walled up.

"But he did a wonderful job of laying out the gardens," says Katherine admiringly. She describes how he planted avenues of graceful palms, and a row of white calla lilies along the south wall, magnificent rosebushes, tall geraniums, bougainvillaea, hibiscus, and the necessary vegetable garden.

With no city water, at first they had to fill tubs with water each night for cooling their transmitters; but very soon, out of appreciation for the station's contribution, the city extended its electricity and water to the HCJB compound. "All Ecuador is witness to the great efforts by HCJB to serve the country in the fullest meaning of the word," they said.

Moore had built a tall tower with a series of slender eucalyptus poles lashed together, topped with a new rotary beam antenna. Finally the night to test the equipment arrived. Jones, who had not yet moved over from Quinta Cornston, got an excited phone call. "Get over here with your camera, C. W. We've got balls of fire, and music on the mountain!"

Clarence rushed over to see four-foot arcs sparking like blue lightning off the antenna ends, floating the music of the station over the countryside.

This was a problem no one had ever encountered, because no one had attempted to put a radio antenna of any kind at a 9600-foot elevation, let alone one so big. People passing the station at night would see this arcing, or round balls glowing at the ends of the antenna terminals, caused by high voltage in the rarified atmosphere. Fascinating pyrotechnic display though it was, the intense heat at the terminal ends was literally melting the antenna.

Moore was stymied. "There has to be a way," he said, going off alone to the coast where he pored over a crate of technical books and prayed. Finally a full understanding of the problem came to him. Back in Quito, Moore mounted copper toilet-bowl floats on the terminals, which virtually eliminated antenna ends and the stunning corona effect. Problem solved.

Moore knew he was on to something, and developed a square of continuous wire backed up by a "parasitic element or re-flector" which then presents a cube shape. Thus was born the "Cubical Quad" which is one of the most popular ham and CB antennas today, and has made HCJB-Quito famous in the world of amateur radio. The Quad was placed on a circular pad which could be turned so as to change the direction of the beam.

(For his work in Ecuador, the government honored Clarence Moore with call letters for life—"HC1JB," for his own ham radio station.)

On Easter Day, 1940, with "a word of applause for foreigners who know how to appreciate the hospitality of our country," expressing "the gratitude of the nation to HCJB with the sincere wish that the station will move along the same path of rectitude to increase its own and Ecuador's fame," President Andres Cordova threw the switch and HCJB's new 10,000-watt trans-mitter was officially on the air: *To fling the gospel around the world.* And it did. Katherine got dizzy opening the letters that began to pour in from Japan, New Zealand, India, Germany—and Russia! Just as the Iron Curtain was coming down.

Leaving the station in the capable hands of Cruz and Aldama, at every opportunity Jones and D. S. Clark would take off with the Radio Rodante. The first sound truck was a wooden struc-ture mounted crudely on a flatbed truck. The drive to the coast was hair-raising and tortuous, especially if they went off the main road into a remote village. In one deep narrow gulley, the sound truck got wedged in tight, with front and rear ends both nosing into the steep incline. C. W. took out a hack-saw, cut a couple of feet off the wooden extension projecting out the rear, and they drove away.

At the Guayas River, C. W. gingerly edged the cumbersome vehicle along the twenty-inch planks onto the bobbing little launch that would take them downriver to Guayaquil. There were no coastal roads, but when the tide was out, they could drive along the hard sand beach, stopping at every little cluster of bamboo huts. Each evening they'd hang up a sheet between two trees, crank up their generator, and roll movies, sometimes educational (which pleased the Ministry and the local schoolmaster), as well as gospel. C. W. would play and D. S. would preach.

The long haul back uphill to Quito was sometimes too much for the eight-gear truck. When the engine heated up, they'd have to stop and put bricks behind the wheels to keep from sliding back down the mountain, and wait till the engine cooled.

They ministered in many of the larger mountain towns. With a special permit from the President which allowed free access anywhere in Ecuador, they would drive into the Plaza where as many as 5000 gathered around in the daytime. For the evening meeting, again the square would be crowded. Everyone showed up: the municipal band, the army band, the mayor to make a speech—and this was all captured by their portable transmitter and broadcast to the rest of Ecuador. They'd show a travelogue and Bible films, preach, and sell Bibles and Testaments, hundreds of them at every stop.

Jones was concerned with "providing baskets for the fruit" they were gathering in. "We cannot, we dare not go on awakening and encouraging interest in the gospel among the people unless somehow we also can nourish and preserve the results. To do less is to be guilty of grossest injustice and inefficiency." Consequently, C. W. constantly worked for closest cooperation with the missionaries to follow up all inquiries, pushing for a strong national church, making plans for a Bible Institute of the Air for those beyond the reach of the church.

But in 1942, C. W. was staying close to home. Marian was very ill. On her way to meet her class of Ecuadorian girls at the little downtown church, Marian had missed the bus. So she had run two miles, most of it uphill. The church was not open, and a tired Marian leaned against the door and fainted, cracking her head on the edge of the gutter as she fell. The men across the road came over to help, but the five little girls wouldn't let them near Marian. But they gave Marian's name and home number.

For the two previous weeks, the telephone had been out of order. And for the two weeks following, it didn't work. Miraculously, this day the call went through. Marian had fractured her skull, and there was a hematoma (mass of blood). She would have to rest.

But Mother was ill—she was expecting a baby again, and there was a houseful of guests. So early one morning Marian got out of bed to help. As she set off down the garden to gather eggs, the old ram came around the corner and butted her. Dick Larson happened to look out the window: "Marian has fallen!" C.W. rushed out with half his face covered in shaving suds and carried his unconscious daughter into the house.

Now Marian was gravely ill. A leading German doctor who was in Quito at the time agreed to take charge. "If we are to dissolve this large hematoma, we must change the body's metabolism. She must have no salt, and no meat. And she must stay absolutely in bed. If you do not follow my orders, she could die at any time."

Katherine got a fixation: "God is going to take Marian; that is why he has given me this new child to carry." Still she struggled on valiantly, trying to cope with Marian's diet on top of the culinary demands imposed by the constant hostessing for HCJB. But one day the doctor came by and found Marian enjoying a chicken leg. He was furious. "But chicken isn't meat, it's fowl," Katherine protested lamely. Adding to Kath's frustrations, following a period of heavy rains, the ceiling came down in Marian's room, spilling plaster over the bed.

Marian's schedule was all off, and she was allowed to do pretty well as she pleased—as long as it was done in bed. One night quite late, as Marian was reading the Sherlock Holmes adventures in *The Hound of the Baskervilles*, she glanced out the window to see the full moon sliding behind dark clouds, and just then the German shepherds began to howl. Suddenly Marian was terrified.

"Through the walls, Daddy heard my whimpering and came in. I don't know how long he sat comforting me," Marian recalls. "But I often hope that I have been as sensitive to the needs of my children as Daddy was."

Marian recovered and the whole family was eagerly looking forward to the new baby. Kath was determined to paint the baby's room, and the smell was asphyxiating. Kath went into early labor.

Clarence took the children to the hospital to see "surely the most beautiful child ever born." But on the third day the baby stopped breathing. There was no oxygen available. Clarence was desperate as he watched the little life petering out. He called the family together and said they should name the child. This was the first time they had seen their father weep, and it frightened them. "He was such a strong man in our eyes." They chose "Elizabeth Pearl."

Later that day Clarence was called to the phone. The children heard a wail and knew that either their mother or the baby had died.

Clarence went alone to the coffinmaker's near the Presidential Plaza, then tenderly carried the small wooden box up the hillside overlooking Quito where they said farewell to little Beth. "I shall never forget Daddy's tears at the graveside of our precious baby sister; we all wanted her so," one daughter recalls with sadness even today. "Daddy never talked about the baby; he loved little children."

There was little time to mourn, however. The world was at war, and news of the American involvement had come to Ecuador during the English Fellowship meeting in the Jones living room.

Young Bob Clark (Stuart's son) was monitoring the radio. A note was slipped to C.W., who excused himself, turning the meeting over to Stuart, and thus heard the first news of Pearl Harbor, which stunned the Western world at 4:00 P.M. EST,

December 7, 1941. Quickly Jones called the U.S. Embassy which had not yet heard of the attack.

C.W. was appointed by the U.S. Embassy to head up Ecuador's Committee of Coordination, traveling throughout the country showing movies and slides of the U.S. military and economic power. C.W. figured he could handle this extra responsibility if he got up an hour earlier and worked a little later each day.

There had been much German infiltration all through South America, but the U.S. still had strongholds in Peru, Ecuador, and Panama. The German bombers would circle Quito, dropping leaflets boasting of what Germany was going to do. Five hundred troops at the German Embassy wearing swastika arm bands marched up and down. C.W. and D.S. laid out evacuation routes with caches of gasoline and food in case they had to get out of Quito.

One day C.W. was told: "We expect a German strike tomorrow. Order your men to shoot their families should there be a takeover." All that day, American P47s flew over Quito, and for some reason, the Germans backed off.

It was a tense time. "Every night we listened to the BBC in England. When Big Ben sounded, we knew that London had not yet fallen," Clarence and Kath recall.

During this period, the NBC network approached HCJB to become "The Voice for Democracy" in South America, a noncommercial affiliate broadcasting a strong schedule of various language programs which NBC sent down on seventeen-inch platters. In appreciation, NBC arranged a gala program in Quito honoring HCJB's twelfth anniversary, featuring Richard Crooks, the star of New York's Metropolitan Opera. NBC also funded a new studio building for the station.

The Jones house now had a steady stream of U.S. Army and Navy boys passing through, who played many boisterous games of pingpong on the dining room table. C.W. was hard to beat, but Katherine's doughnuts made up for any defeats. Their young Ecuadorian friends loved to join them. "This is the only place we have any fun," they'd say.

During the war, in spite of restraints, word kept trickling through that the powerful new voice of HCJB was being heard. An airman flying a mission toward Japan, tuning in to his base was astonished to hear the voice of his pastor back in the States broadcasting their church service over Quito's HCJB. From Sumatra, from Sweden, from the high Arctic of Alaska and Canada, Christians were being encouraged and souls saved.

Normally, a 10,000-watt station would not be able to broadcast over such distances. The explanation for this came at a 1943 international meeting of radio technicians in New York City to which Clarence Moore was invited. Here he was greeted with compliments for HCJB. "What a smart operation, to put a radio station on the equator, the very finest location for north-south broadcasting! With equal distance from the magnetic poles, it's the one place in the world freest from atmospheric disturbance. And with your 100-foot tower sitting on a 9600-foot mountain, you virtually have a 10,000-foot antenna. The higher above sea level you can get your tower, the farther the signal will travel. Amazing how your engineers could have chosen the best site on earth!"

Not quite what the experts had told C.W. in 1930. "We knew all along it had to be the best, because it was God's choice," C.W. rejoiced. "It's nice that technology finally has caught up."

It's amazing
what can be
accomplished
if you don't worry
about who gets
the credit.
C.W. Jones

Assured that the station indeed was reaching "to the uttermost part of the earth," the next step, as C.W. saw it, was to add more languages to the station's programming so that these untold multitudes could hear the gospel in their own tongue.

Reuben Larson was joined in the Swedish broadcasting by a lovely Swedish girl who had married the Ecuadorian Consul in Chicago and then had come home with him to Quito. So appreciated were her broadcasts that twice the King of Sweden has decorated Ellen Campaña.

Peter Deyneka of the Slavic Gospel Association preached the first Russian gospel program. German, Portuguese, Japanese, and French were all added, as were Yiddish, Italian, Dutch, and Czechoslovakian, with the help of missionaries and other Quito visitors prevented from returning to their homeland during war time. Consequently, at one point during the war HCJB was broadcasting in eighteen languages, with five transmissions going out simultaneously. As well, a "Service Stripes Hour" with military music and the gospel was dedicated to servicemen around the world. The Red Cross in New York used HCJB to relay messages from home.

In 1945, the staff of HCJB numbered fifteen missionaries and sixty nationals. During the next ten years, it exploded to eighty-seven missionaries and over 100 nationals.

Jones had recruited most new personnel as he toured missionary conventions and summer conferences, playing fast sets of tennis and sitting by the lake long into the night talking with prospective candidates. "First there should be total commitment to God, then to a country, and finally to a mission," he'd advise.

"What are the requirements for an HCJB missionary?" he'd be asked. C.W. would reply, "You must be a specialist in one or two areas, and very good in several others." Once they were accepted, he'd tell them to "bring along a tuxedo to meet the president and overalls to do whatever work comes to hand."

Often on these swings through the States and Canada, Clarence would be joined by his brother Howard with his trumpet. They were together in Chicago's Orchestra Hall for Torrey Johnson's first Saturday night Youth For Christ rally. Jones remembers their peeking around the curtains just a few minutes before the scheduled hour, and their hearts sank. There were only fifteen or twenty people in that big auditorium. But by the time the program commenced, the place was packed. (Billy Graham was the relatively unknown speaker of the evening.)

One night as Howard and Clarence were driving along in a blizzard, suddenly C.W. felt compelled to stop the car right in the middle of the highway. And the next moment, scarcely six feet in front of their stopped vehicle, like a ghost in the silent whiteness, a train swooshed past. The astonished pair again could only praise God for his unmistakable guidance, the unfailing "Divine Radar."

On the field, Clarence Jones was absolutely relentless, even ruthless in his determination for excellence—"tyrannical, totalitarian," some criticized. He would accept no excuse for staff being late for rehearsals, for an assigned task not done. "Come floods or torrential rains, you wouldn't dare not perform!"

Jones demanded the best. He simply would not tolerate incompetence or anything slipshod. His own daughter Marjorie remembers praying fervently that the Lord would come before she had to accompany her father's trombone solo on the little reed organ. But then Marjorie admits that she was the one who hated to practice. C.W. was known to pull her from the program when she wasn't playing well.

"You're not fair, Daddy," Marian chided in defense of her little sister. C.W. took her aside, and speaking as one adult to another, explained his side of the story, why Marjorie could not be allowed to shirk her duties, for her sake or the Mission's.

"A good decision is worth sticking by, even when friends disagree," was one of Jones's proverbs.

Always "fierce to defend the integrity of the Mission," C.W. kept a close watch on all programming, sometimes going right down into the studio and snatching a distasteful record from the turntable to smash it across the edge of a desk. (HCJB has a written policy for its music.) If someone began to talk about politics, he'd signal the control operator to cut the microphone and put on a record. The speaker would never know.

There was an almost military command to the way he ran the station. "When the Captain walked into the room, you snapped to attention," early staff recall. Yet they knew he asked nothing of them that he would not do himself. "We all worked like crazy people on programs, and C.W. worked just as hard along with us. If he left, we knew it was never to goof off, but to work at something else." When they decided to keep the station going all night, broadcasting around the clock to take advantage of prime-time listening around the world, Jones was first to volunteer for the "hoot owl" shift. He had a sense of urgency "to use every God-given minute of the night and day."

Jones always impressed on newcomers that they were guests, privileged to enjoy the hospitality of a progressive, forward-looking government in the most beautiful country on earth. "We have no rights. We must be understanding and agreeable." Their deportment, on or off the station, was to be impeccable. He cautioned the women on their response to these charming Latins, and told the men, "Hands off all but your wife!" ("I got sickened at the Chicago Tab by the way some of these visiting evangelists would paw the girls," Jones explains.) He was a model of gallantry, always courteous, a perfect gentleman, but very careful in his dealings with the opposite sex.

He encouraged HCJB missionaries to take part in community life, joining civic clubs, teaching at the university or music conservatory. "We are here to minister to every strata of society." He counseled them against making any comments about the country or its people for at least six months, to reserve judgment on the mission and its procedures until they had put in the first year; and he urged them, out of all fairness to the churches who had funded their coming to Ecuador, to stick out that difficult first term.

It wasn't easy to mesh a group of prima donna soloists with a working team, Jones will admit. The people coming to HCJB were all highly trained specialists—professionals, musicians, soloists, and artists—in their own right.

But Jones had had good training when only a youngster with the nineteen professional musicians in Chicago. And he was a big man, totally committed to seeking after God and to the mission. "It's amazing what can be accomplished if you don't worry about who gets the credit," he'd say as he plunged into one new project after another, always looking for ways to bring out the best in a person, to "stretch them," to help them excel and take a place of leadership. He had an uncanny ability to assess people, and he trusted them as well as his judgment.

All agree that people were most important to C.W., not just "important people," but the shy new missionaries, the Indians, everyone. He always had time to speak to Felipe at the Gate House and shake his hand.

"C.W. and Mrs. Jones really cared about each member of the family," staff say. "They'd do anything for you. C.W. would be up in the middle of the night to meet your plane or train. He was always warm and friendly, gracious and courteous at all times, joking but always in good taste. He has a presence that makes you aware of him as soon as he walks into a room. Clarence Jones just naturally is a 'take-charge' person. He could overwhelm you."

Certainly C.W. was admired and respected by all, but the remoteness, the aloneness, the discipline that must accompany

effective leadership prevented his having a warm, loving relationship with all but his peers and family. Yet people who
remember Jones from the early days say that "with his dedication, his ability to express himself, his burden for the world, we
considered him to be the embodiment of everything a missionary should be."

Wherever he was, things moved. "He helped with everything,
and he was the best in everything he did," coworkers agree.
For all this tremendous energy, this seeming tirelessness, C.W.
took time out for recreation and rest, and insisted that the
others do the same. "And this time is not to be spent in
devotions or study," he'd tell new recruits. "The Christian
worker has to have as much fun, as much playing of games as
possible. When you go before the microphone, you must
sound victorious, even if you have a toothache or a backache.
It's true that you must be anointed by the Spirit of God, but you
have to keep yourself in shape. Life can't be all seriousness,
discipline, and music. There must be fun."

C.W. set an example with his vacations at the ocean, going off
on evangelistic trips with D.S., taking little breaks with Kath
visiting missionaries in Otavalo and elsewhere in the country.

"You must have a break each week if you are going to be
fresh," he insisted. So every Monday they shut down the
station—"lunatics," the nationals called them, (*lunes* is Spanish
for "Monday")—and all piled into a bus with picnic lunches for
a day of baseball and football games and races of all kinds.

"The way those buses hurtled around the narrow mountain
roads!" staff remember wonderingly. "Sometimes the bus
would lurch to a halt, the gears would grind, and then she'd
begin to slip; everyone would hold his breath and pray that we
wouldn't all slide back over the precipice. If anything happened
to that bus, the whole mission would have been wiped out on
the spot!"

Volleyball with the nationals and missionaries was a fun part
of every day (not playing against each other, but integrated
departmental teams). The Fourth of July, Thanksgiving, and
Christmas were celebrated with great gusto, with the American

colony invited out to share in the festivities—the races and games, the platters of fried chicken and potato salad served at long tables under the palm trees. Around the world today, many Americans treasure memories of carols sung on Christmas Eve around the Christmas tree (actually three scrawny pines lashed together to make a fairly presentable whole) with a microphone dangling from the studio window to catch the music and the message of Immanuel—"Hoy Cristo Jesús Bendice"—and float it "to the uttermost parts of the earth."

Broadcasts were done from some unusual places: from Dos Ríos, for instance, where a relay station was hooked up in the church of Indian believers; and from a DC-3 flying over Quito, as Pan American Airways celebrated its twenty-thousandth flight across the equator. For many years, their pilots used HCJB's radio beam to guide their dangerous descent through the jumble of mountains into Quito.

Mail was coming in weekly from remote areas, with a few francs enclosed from France, a bagful of pennies from Eskimos at Tuktoyaktuk on the Arctic Ocean. "We had nineteen listeners on our first day. Now we have nineteen million receivers within HCJB's listening radius," C.W. reported.

"More audience equals more programming equals more staff equals more funds." With this simple equation, Jones decided they should have a proper office in the U.S. rather than just a receipt-issuing post. It was decided that he and Reuben Larson would alternate, spending two years in the States and two years in Quito to represent the mission adequately in North America.

This was feasible with the strong leadership that had emerged on the field. Added to Larson's ability as a superb evangelist having unusual rapport with Latin Americans, D.S. Clark had also joined the HCJB staff, and he was a fine representative of the mission. Tall and distinguished in appearance, with his background of British gentility (his uncle had been governor of the Island of Jamaica), with the finesse an international education brings, Stuart Clark was at ease in any situation, turning up at official functions in the presidential palace looking elegant in top hat and tails, carrying off his role with magnificent aplomb.

Paul Young was another who could go anywhere and meet anyone. John Clark, too, had won a special place in the hearts of Ecuadorians, and was perhaps the most loved of all missionaries.

Leaving this fine complement of outstanding ability in Quito, Jones took his family to the red brick duplex in Flushing, New York, and launched a great push for personnel and funds for HCJB.

But here again, Clarence Jones was marked by the bigness of his vision. Vergil Gerber recalls the missionary conference where instead of presenting the needs of HCJB, Jones zeroed in on the needs of the other missions represented, and unfolded the Scriptures to promote worldwide missionary interests, not even mentioning the Voice of the Andes. "Here was a man of deep and genuine humility who was not out to promote his own interests, but rather was a model of the Scripture, 'in honor preferring one another.'"

Clarence Jones
was God's man
in God's place
in God's time.
Vergil Gerber

Although Jones's calling had been to Ecuador, his burden always
had been for a lost world, and in spite of turning down
LeTourneau's offer to support him in a far-east outreach, the
vision never seemed to dim. Constantly he was casting about
for ways to increase gospel broadcasting worldwide.

In a historic meeting, April 15, 1944, in Columbus, Ohio,
under the chairmanship of his old friend Howard Ferrin,
Clarence brought together the top missionary leaders to meet
with the top radio pastors. "It's difficult to develop missionary
radio among those who have never *used* radio." he figured. This
led to the forming of the World Conference on Missionary
Radio, which later became the International Christian Broadcasters.

"I don't know of anyone who could have pulled the international organizations involved together as did Clarence Jones,"
says Bob Bowman, president of the Far East Broadcasting
Company. "We all looked to Dr. Jones as the sort of 'dean' of
international Christian broadcasters." "C.W. took great joy in
the achievements of others in Christian radio, even when they
seemed to get a jump on HCJB," a coworker marveled.

In 1946, Jones began holding Summer Schools of Christian
Radio, first in Providence, Rhode Island, then the Bible Insti-

tute of Los Angeles and Moody Bible Institute of Chicago as well. C.W. was always forward-thinking, suggesting to the mission that they get into FM "to have the jump on everyone else in the country." He saw television as the coming tool for airwaves evangelism. "Like a kid with a new toy," he brought a black-and-white TV into the office one day. At home, a TV was set up in the dining room, and the children resented its interrupting their pleasant mealtimes while Dad "was glued to the tube doing research."

Jones's ministry as an "encourager" to other full-time workers began evidencing itself during these years, with God using a brief word from his lips to build up others in the body of Christ. A colleague shared how at an Urbana Conference, in the midst of a very busy program of activities, "C.W. took time to tell me how significantly God was blessing my ministry, and more than anything else at that time, I needed that encouragement."

Gerber sums up: "To so many of us in the ministry, he wasn't simply 'Mr. Missionary Radio.' Clarence Jones was *God's man in God's place in God's time.* He was a man who truly walked with God."

When he'd get back into the office following one of his junkets, Norma Cuthbertson, HCJB's secretary in New York, tells how he would go through his mail. "Now, do you have any problems?" he'd ask. "I can give you all the time you want, as long as it isn't more than five minutes!"

Actually all six secretaries who served under Jones over the years agree C.W. was a joy to work with. Sometimes they'd come in to find he'd already typed a stack of letters by 7:30 A.M. "He could keep three secretaries going!"

"C.W. knew how to conserve his secretary's time by thinking through what he had to say before calling you in for dictation," Ruth Clark Christiansen maintains. "I was always impressed by his efficiency, his fairness, and his ability to inspire others. He inspired me much beyond my capabilities."

Muggs Poole liked his great sense of humor, his journalistic flow of words, his computer mind for recall. "And he had such a nice way of showing appreciation," Muggs says. She had just returned from her father's funeral and a letter was waiting from C.W. "The sea was as calm as Muggs's nerves in the office . . ." he wrote. "There seemed to be no area where this brilliant man was not most knowledgeable," Muggs concluded.

Betty Willison recalls how C.W. would give her a pile of dictation and then stand behind her while she typed. "I can't work with you watching." "I'm so sorry," he'd say. "C.W. knew how to apologize," Betty says.

"Certainly he was stern and exacting, a stickler for details," Betty concludes. "But he was not a nitpicker. He knew which details were important. One day I typed sixteen letters with his wife's name spelled with a 'C.' He signed them all, then quietly said, 'Next time, could you please spell it with a "K"?'

"He knew how to correct, but graciously. He expected, demanded excellence. He taught me so much. But most of all, I felt he was my friend; he cared about my sick husband. He'd speak to him on the phone, and visit him; he'd talk to my Italian-speaking father who almost no one else attempts to communicate with."

But most of Jones's time was spent out of the office. One trip took him away for months while he toured South America. During this period Katherine had gotten used to giving orders around the house, and when C.W. came back and started "laying down the law" to the youngsters who were getting away with too much, Katherine was upset.

She flounced off to enroll in night classes at City College, studying radio production and script writing. But Kath knew more about the subject than her professor. "You can teach me and the class," he protested. So much for Katherine's fling at women's lib.

Marian had stayed in Quito following high school graduation, having obtained work as a secretary at the U.S. Embassy. Once, when Marian had come to New York on a visit, on Sunday morning, to Marian's horror, her mother came down the stairs wearing bright red lipstick. And makeup! Marian nearly fell over. No one in Quito wore makeup. Mother was going to the devil! Then, when they went off to a sedate, rather stuffy Presbyterian Church, the strongly evangelical Marian was even more horrified. "My dear one, you can hear Christ speaking in every sermon if you only listen," was Marian's sermon for the day.

Grandmother Emma Jones had also come to live with them following George's death, and this made for a rather difficult time. She was having severe headaches and the children remember how she would be curt with them. In her eyes, Clarence could do no wrong and had never done any wrong, and she constantly held up this image in front of them. "It was impossible to please her," they recall.

This would not have helped young Dick who was having a struggle with his own identity, "as do all sons of high-achieving fathers," according to Dr. Henry Brandt. Dick was a straight-A student, a well coordinated athlete, a skilled mountaineer who was offered a spot on the American team to climb Mount Everest, and an excellent vocalist and trombonist. Still he struggled with desperate feelings of inadequacy and low self-esteem.

One spring day, he simply did not come home from classes at Queen's College. Kath was frantic. Was he in the river? Had he been hurt? They called all the hospitals. They called the police: "Thousands of eighteen-year-old kids leave home, ma'am."

The days stretched into weeks and months. It was a time of strain in their marriage, and a time of intense soul-searching for Clarence. Had he been too strict with Dick? Had he demanded too much excellence? Had he driven his son over the brink?

Clarence began to search the Scriptures for God's role for fathers, noting that God had made the father a priest and a king: a king to be the authority figure, to take time to instruct and discipline. ". . . with the loving discipline the Lord himself approves, with suggestions and godly advice" (Eph. 6:4, TLB). "Fathers, don't overcorrect your children or make it difficult for them to obey the commandments" (Eph. 6:4, Phillips). As well, Jones noted that the father is to be a priest, to lead the family in worship and spiritual growth, and to be a counselor and provider.

Jones's struggles are reflected in his notes. "If a father is to assume his essential role as head of the house, first he must *evaluate himself* in honesty and humilty, to face up to his own strengths and weaknesses. Then he must *evaluate the marital factors*—the factors that promote harmonious family living. Evaluate the *children factors*—'children are people—they do grow up.' And his fourth searching question: *Are any dependants living under the same roof?* How do they affect family routine? Are they overshadowing the wife or husband or children? And finally, what goals, purposes, ambitions do I hold for my family? What are the major interests for each family member? *How can a father prepare himself mentally, physically, spiritually for a family unity program?*" Again the children say simply, "Father chose to allow God to change him."

At last a young friend appeared on Katherine's doorstep with a postcard from Dick. He was in Dallas. Clarence was away again, so Kath, together with Chet and Ruth, and Marian who was now married to Stuart Clark's son Bob—all five set out, driving night and day.

Marian and Bob went with Kath up the steps to the boarding house. "He should be home any minute," they were told. Just then Dick came along on his motorcycle, and hugged his mother as if he'd never let her go again.

A year later, enrolled in Wheaton College, Dick sent a birthday greeting home to his father:

Dec. 11, 1951, from son Dick
On occasion of father's birthday, Dec. 15.

I'm really proud that my Dad is one who all his life
has never stopped atop the summit of a mountain of success,
but breathing deep of sweet fresh air
has plunged anew in toil and hardships,
and found even greater triumph there.
And greatest thing of all, I think,
is that this work was not just done
for earth's short useless joys,
but for our God, the triune power.

The thoughts I've thought, the prayers I've prayed,
are products of the base you laid.
For health, for joys, you've always paid.
Your love my attributes have bought.

May I through all this life to come,
run half as well and half as far;
may God's will be my life's whole sum
and so to follow in your path,
removing from God's final wrath
some who know not what they are.

And so again my love I send,
A love which nothing e'er can rend.
To one who's been much more than Dad:
The BESTEST Pal I ever had!
Your son,
Dick

(poem enclosed)

The hero of my childhood days,
My friend and pal in countless ways,
No word can quite describe his worth,
My Dad—the swellest man on earth.

With more love than words can ever tell.
Your son,
Dick

We'll never
win the war
with one gun;
we must get
a whole barrage
up there!
C.W. Jones

On his deputation work, Clarence Jones was a frequent visitor in the Peoples Church, Toronto, Canada. (Oswald Smith never let him forget the time he hadn't showed up for their midweek meeting.) Under C. W.'s ministry there, Paul Roberts, a young medical student, committed his life to missionary service.

Jones sent off a note to Reuben Larson: "I've been thinking about the need to have our own medical staff in Quito. A resident doctor could: (a) oversee the health of our growing staff; (b) operate a small Indian clinic; (c) carry on an itinerant work with the sound bus; (d) give medical advice on the radio. We might also install a small hospital for missionaries and the public.

"If you like the idea, Reu, I think we have just the man who would be supported by Peoples Church."

This was no hastily conceived idea. Clarence had been simmering it for years. He'd see the Indians coming down the Pan American highway just a block from the station with their loads of wood and carnations to sell at the market; then often they'd be robbed and beaten on their way home, kicked, buffeted about. "Our hearts went out to them because so many were sick and emaciated. Nobody seemed to care for them and they couldn't get into hospitals. The Lord laid it on our hearts to do something."

C. W. was astounded to discover that in fifty years of missions, Ecuador had not had a Christian doctor. He went from mission to mission pleading with them to begin a medical ministry.

Clarence talked it over with Katherine: "Our calling is to radio. But here is this need, and everyone is turning us down. Does that mean we are to get involved?"

Finally HCJB decided to rent a little house on the Pan Am highway. They cleaned it up and installed Dr. Paul Roberts and nurse Kathleen Erb, with Marjorie Jones joining them the following year after graduation from nurse's training in New York.

They were there in time to help with the devastating earthquake at Ambato that left 6000 dead and 100,000 homeless. On Friday, August 5, 1949, in the late afternoon Clarence Jones received a phone call from President Galo Plaza: Could the HCJB medical team go down? Of course. Quickly they sped over the seventy-five miles, followed by the sound bus. At 6:30 A.M. the next morning, the president, from HCJB's sound bus, called on the nation for relief to the stricken area.

On Sunday, Jones had a cable from NBC in New York: Could they arrange a direct contact? So that afternoon, the president, weary himself from digging people out of the ruins, told the world of the total destruction of some areas, through an HCJB hookup with NBC, CBS, and Mutual networks. C. W. had another call from New York: Can you get us some film to show on TV? "Sure," C. W. replied, and before dawn on Monday morning, Bob Clark and the HCJB film crew were on their way. The government used HCJB's radio equipment to keep in communication with the site. J. D. Clark was in charge of relocating the orphaned children; HCJB carpenters built pre-fab houses and sent them down, and D. S. coordinated the whole effort, pitching in as front-line helpers in their adopted country's time of crisis.

Harry Rimmer, the noted Bible teacher, had become involved

in the medical ministry of HCJB. He and C. W. had met at several conferences, and one day Rimmer asked Jones, "What can we do for you that no one else wants to do?" "Why, the medical," Jones quickly replied. At that point, Jones had just rented the clinic, so the timing was just right. Rimmer still had his painter's union card, and back in Los Angeles, he walked along the street till he came to a house that needed painting; then he went up to the door and wangled the job. The next Sunday in his young people's Bible class at First Presbyterian Church, Rimmer announced, "This is what I have done. Now it's your turn." Then he went on to George Palmer's "Morning Cheer" radio program in Philadelphia and raised funds there, first to purchase the clinic and then to build a new hospital in Quito.

During the Joneses' stints in Quito, Katherine had an increasing stream of missionaries coming and going. It seemed that everyone made their way to the jungle via the Joneses' guest house ("Jeremiah 33:3" they dubbed it). Once Jim Elliott was staying with them, and C. W. brought a new missionary named Betty home from the train. "That was all they needed," the Joneses recall fondly of Jim and Betty Elliott.

Kath had ample opportunity to practice her own special healing ministry. At every sprained ankle or sinus infection or what have you, out would come Kath's "little black bag," packed with homeopathic herbs and treatments which had been introduced to her by Dr. Wilfred Tidmarsh when he had come up from Peru to speak on the radio. Little by little, he taught Katherine the basics of homeopathy. When little Joel Van Der Puy's arm got caught in the wringer, Kath went right over with pills to swallow and a rub for the arm, and there was no swelling or bruising, to his mother's amazement. When the whole medical staff came down with hepatitis, Kath set up a sick bay in the guest house, and treated them all with her little pills.

Under Clarence's jurisdiction, the Bible Institute of the Air was meeting the need for discipling the Spanish Christians, a need which had long concerned Jones. Furthermore, their own Spanish print shop had been set up.

Just as they had not intended to get into medical work, Jones had not anticipated church planting, but the need of the English-speaking community could not be avoided, so those early Bible studies and hymn sings in their and the D.S. Clark's living rooms had grown into the English Fellowship Church, where Clarence directed the music and shared the pastoring with D.S.

The school which Jones had started for the Christian nationals' children he had turned over to the Covenant Church and they were doing a fine job with it.

The Radio Circle ministry was mushrooming. The first pre-tuned listening posts were just five-by-six-by-eight-inch boxes with the Voice of the Andes symbol on the front, two or three tubes, depending on how far they were from the station, and no tuning dial, simply an on-off switch. These were fastened on a wall, with an antenna wire strung between two trees running down to the set. The missionary would go around to check them every two or three months and this was a fruitful contact.

Then an HCJB engineer, Marion Krekler, dreamed up a mouse-trap-size crystal set with a coil, a crystal, and a few connecting wires mounted on a three-by-five block of wood; and again pre-tuned to HCJB. These were mass-produced in a shop on the compound. The first 125 sets were loaned within a five-mile radius, then another 200 went out, finally 13,000 were in use and still 900 were on the waiting list. These novelties were a special delight to the innovative Clarence.

Whether on these tiny pre-tuned crystal sets, or the shiny stainless steel Scott radios that Jones had sold to wealthy landowners, all over Ecuador people were listening, and lives were being changed. The power of HCJB programs was brought home vividly to a prominent member of Congress as he visited a hacienda in the country one Sunday afternoon. To his astonishment, the Indian peons gathered around the porch. "Please, may we listen to the radio now?"

The congressman was astonished on two counts: first that they were sober, because it was accepted that on Sunday the

Indians got drunk; and second, that they wanted to listen to the radio—"They have no mind for this," he protested.

"Ah, but Señora Ochoa speaks to us in our Quichua language." The visitor was impressed as they sat quietly, listening to the broadcast, and then graciously took their leave.

"Now they'll go and get drunk," the congressman was sure. "I've got to follow these fellows." But at their homes, he found them happy and contented, with their children clean and neatly dressed.

He returned to the hacienda owner: "What makes the difference? Why are they not off getting drunk?" His host replied: "It's the Voice of the Andes. I don't know what they talk about, but whatever it is, it changes them to the kind of people you just saw. I wish that many more would listen."

This was of special interest to the congressman, because President Galo Plaza had put before Congress the request to renew the twenty-five-year license for HCJB. (Galo Plaza had come to Clarence: "I want to do something for you." "OK," Jones had replied. "Renew our contract for us.") One of the communist members was protesting vigorously. A group of Catholic women had stormed into Congress demanding, "Whatever you do for the Voice of the Andes, you must do for us. We want a radio station."

The congressman replied, "Whenever you do anything as good for Ecuador as the Voice of the Andes, you can have help."

So out of appreciation for HCJB's contribution to the country, Congress renewed their contract in January, 1948, eight years in advance.

Once again Jones was rejoicing in this miracle. "Undoubtedly the anointing of the Lord was upon Clarence Jones that he would be held in such high esteem by government officials, and enjoy such favor in a land where evangelicals were often oppressed," a fellow missionary observes. Assured of another twenty-five years of broadcasting, C.W. felt free to bring in more power for a stronger voice—50,000 watts. Here again, the radio laws Clarence had helped write for Ecuador caught up with him. With that kind of power, they'd have to go even farther out of town. And they were looking at acres of antennas now.

For three years, Jones, D.S. Clark, and Francisco Cruz scoured the countryside. Finally they found forty-five acres on a main road, just twenty two miles from Quito. It was cheap, and it had the water they needed to cool the diesel generators. Within three days they had bought it. Bob Wittig, an HCJB engineer, purchased the adjoining fifty acres: "You might need it someday," he said.

Jones and son-in-law Bob Clark were on the job at 6 A.M. every morning, up on the tractor and bulldozer clearing the cornfield. Bob had studied architecture, so he supervised the burnt brick construction.

C.W. had to leave town, and the job of transfering the transmitting and generating operation began to bog down. According to Bob, "the whole thing would still be in Quito if C.W. had not come back, looked it over, and announced, 'Next Saturday we move.' And they did."

"Jones overwhelmed people with the moves he would make when he saw they had to be done," George Poole commented after twenty-five years with HCJB. "Like this move to Pifo. He had to clear the fields. There was no electricity. They had to build a generating plant, and get water. There was so much work involved. But if something needed to be done, and Jones decided it was right, 'Let's go,' he'd say, and make the move. Jones is totally goal-oriented. He's never stopped by a problem."

Jones never saw this as anything special. "When you sit down to build a tower or anything, it's just the story of Luke 14:28. First there is the *decision*—that you intend to build; then there is the *deliberation* of counting the cost; finally there is the *determination* to finish it. It's as simple as that," he says.

"But special insight has to have been given to C.W. because he's right most of the time. The rest of us bat 60 percent and figure we're doing well," Poole concludes.

"He was always jumps ahead of everyone else," Bob Savage remembers. Jones had seen Pifo's new "specially designed 'curtain' antennas" shortly after the war at Canada's overseas shortwave installation, and had promptly fired off a memo for HCJB engineers to get ready to dump their "outmoded rhombics." C.W. brought back the details and they were in business.

During one of their turns in the States, Paul Young's brother John called to say he'd be in New York; could he stay with them? "Come right along," Katherine responded hospitably.

When John came out to breakfast next morning, having spent the night on pillows from the davenport laid on the floor, he said, "You people from the Voice of the Andes are going to have a decent place with guest rooms." The Flushing quarters were crowded, and getting about New York presented some problems for the girls working with them. A few days later John Young called Clarence: "I've got just the place for you."

Adam Welty went along to look. "What do you think, Dad?" Clarence asked. "I think it's just all right for the Lord's children." So the stately homestead on four-and-one-half acres in Talcottville, fifteen miles west of Hartford, Connecticut, was purchased for $11,000, with seventeen rooms and a three-car garage, beautiful reception and living rooms, and curving walnut staircase (just right for a bride, Katherine was thinking). The garage could be made into offices, and Kath was looking forward to entertaining the candidates and missionaries in the new home. They could take possession in February 1953.

He is no fool
who gives up
what he cannot keep
to gain that
which he cannot lose!
Jim Elliott

On January 12, Clarence and Katherine had finished meetings on the West Coast and were headed back across the States in the new car they had just purchased. Still in California, Katherine was knitting as Clarence slowed the car to turn in for gas. At that same time, the car in the oncoming lane slowed down to make a turn; the car following him pulled out to go around, and suddenly saw the Joneses' car approaching in the same lane. He swerved, trying desperately to hit the ditch, but instead he smashed head-on into Clarence and Katherine. The couple in the other car were killed instantly.

Clarence hit the steering wheel with his chin, pushing it through the windshield, crushing his jaw like an eggshell; his chest, too, was crushed. The engine came up against Katherine's feet, twisting the toes around to touch her heels; several ribs were broken. Blood was gushing from a hole in her forehead the size of a half-dollar as the ambulance attendants dragged her from the wreck. "She's dead," Kath heard them say. "How wonderful!" she thought. "Now I'll see the Lord." Then she fell unconscious.

Clarence, somehow, never lost consciousness. Always one to plan ahead for any foreseeable emergency, he had turned off the key, and by the time the ambulance had arrived, had managed to scribble on a piece of paper Romans 8:28: "All things work together for good to them that love God." He handed this to the attendants as they lifted him from the wreck. When they tried to lay him down, Jones communicated that he must remain upright. Had he not, he would have choked on his own blood, doctors later said.

In the Santa Barbara hospital the doctor stopped counting after forty-two as he threaded the broken bits of Clarence's jawbone on wire.

Still on the critical list, Clarence wrote on a piece of paper, "Where's Katherine?" They moved a cot for Clare into Kath's room so they could be together for her last days.

One of the finest plastic surgeons happened to be in Santa Barbara en route to Hawaii, and he closed up the hole in Kath's head. But the brain damage shown on the EEG was so massive that they hoped she would never regain consciousness. "She would always see double, and she'll never be able to think or feed herself again," they told C. W. "And we would have to amputate both mangled feet." A cable was sent to Quito: "Pray!"

Nine days later, Kath began to float back to consciousness. She heard someone shushing her. "That's strange," she thought. "I'm in heaven and surely the Lord wouldn't shush me." Then she opened her eyes and looked across at Clarence—two eyes in a face swollen and black as ebony, head swathed in bandages, wires sticking out both sides of his jaw. "Why, you're not the Lord!" she exclaimed, and slipped away again.

And then Dick walked into the room and put his arms around her. First Sergeant Richard Jones, "Korean war hero," wounded once and the holder of three battle stars, a member of the hard-hitting Fifth Combat Team who had established a record of 150 consecutive days in battle with the Chinese communists, "plucked from the front lines" and flown home to march in President Eisenhower's inaugural parade. Arriving in New York, Dick had learned of the accident, and two hours later was on an airliner for California.

Dick accompanied his parents on their flight to New York's

Presbyterian Medical Center for further surgery on C. W.'s jaw.

The plane stopped at Chicago where Lillian and Howard came aboard with Nancy, a freshman at Wheaton College. Kath, now conscious, head bandaged, both legs in casts, cried and wailed. She didn't want Nancy to leave. The crew let Nancy back on the plane for a few minutes, and then had to take off. Returning to the dorm, Nancy was so distraught that the girls took up a collection to pay her airfare to New York so she could be with her parents.

Dick stopped off for a brief visit in Wheaton with his college sweetheart, Carol Jean Carlson, the daughter of the two missionaries who had touched Clare and Kath's lives at Lake Harbor all those years ago. Carol Jean had been born to them after that, and the two young people had met at Wheaton College before Dick went off to Korea.

In New York, the surgeon worked on Clarence's jaw. "I don't see how you'll ever be able to talk, let alone blow a horn again," he told C. W. Carlton Booth and Jack Wyrtzen visited Clarence as he sucked up baby food through a straw, somehow communicating to them that through it all, he was indeed claiming Romans 8:28.

"Through all the years I have never seen Clarence when his attitude was anything but optimistic," Booth marveled.

"This is a great way to get publicity for HCJB," Wyrtzen kidded him. "Everybody's praying for you." It was a red-letter day at the hospital when they took out the skewers and told Kath, "Your husband can move his jaw."

On February 22, good old Chet and Ruth were at the hospital to pick up the Joneses and drive them to Talcottville, stopping at the first Howard Johnson's for C. W.'s favorite Swiss chocolate almond ice cream. They'd closed up their own place and come to New York to get the house ready and take care of Kath and Clarence.

Katherine had two walking casts, and was strongly sedated. She was recovering, but slowly. Already, though, her progress was miraculous. Clarence was determined to get his jaws

working again. With the stick-to-it-iveness of the German and
the stubbornness of his English ancestry, each day he exercised
until he couldn't stand the pain. After a brief rest, he'd go at it
again. "It hurt just to watch him grimacing and struggling,"
Katherine remembers.

Before long, the clenched teeth would open enough for him
to talk. Then one day in May, there was a shout from the top of
the stairs: "Kath, I can whistle!"

"That told me my face and jaw muscles were really working,"
C. W. says. "Maybe I would play a horn again. . . ."

By August he was able to keep his summer conference
engagements, but called in brother Howard for the music. At
Gull Lake, he introduced Howard with flourish; then Howard
stood up and said, "I'm not playing unless you play with me!"
C. W. happened to have his trombone along, hoping that
before the summer was ended, he would be able to blow. "Here
goes," he grinned as Howard's wife, Lillian, swung into "Stars
and Stripes Forever."

And Clarence blew that trombone again, maybe not the
sweet tones that rang over the Venezuelan mountain or across
Chicago's Soldier Field years earlier, but the sweetest sound
Clarence had ever heard. It all came back; Clarence and Howard
made several recordings after that, the last in 1965.

Katherine's recovery was slower. For months it was as if she
were rebelling against being returned to this world, sometimes
refusing to accept that she was not with her Lord but was in
Connecticut with her family. Clarence pleaded with her. The
children pleaded with her: "Mother, we need you. Please don't
wish to leave us." After four months Katherine announced,
"I'm not taking any more of those pain killers." There was no
addiction, and her mind began to clear.

Still, all day she just lay on the chaise lounge looking out the
window. Ruth insisted she take part in activities: "Come on
Kath, we're going for a drive now," or, "Would you help me
fold the clothes?" One day in July Ruth suggested that Kath
might make a cherry pie; it took Kath almost four hours. When
Marian came home a year later, Katherine drove the fifteen

miles to Hartford to meet their train, the first time she had had the car out alone. Marian was impatient with her Mother's dawdling, taking so long to get the lunch ready, when suddenly it dawned on her: "Mother is extending herself. This is still very hard for her to do."

But she was walking quite well. When her father came to see her a few weeks after the accident, he looked at Kath and beamed "You have your feet! Satan told me you would lose them, but I talked to God. . . ." And Katherine was able to hostess a lovely reception when Marjorie was the lovely bride walking down that curving walnut staircase.

On their next trip to Quito, the Joneses stopped in Panama to visit with Howard and Lillian who were heading up the radio station which HCJB had taken over, ministering to the ships of the world as they came through the Canal Zone. In Quito, the Rimmer Memorial Hospital was opened in October 1955. Mrs. Rimmer came down for the dedication. (Harry Rimmer died just before its completion; Mrs. Rimmer visited several times after that, staying with Katherine in the guest house.)

Kath and Clare pitched in to help. With a book on hospital administration propped open on the desk, Clarence ran the business and maintenance end; Kath took charge of the kitchen and laundry, thus freeing Dr. Roberts for nursing and medical duties.

Down in the jungles of Shell Mera, five young men who were preparing to take the gospel to the savage Auca tribe, were pleading with HCJB to build a hospital for the Indians of the vast Amazon basin. "We don't know how to run this place yet," C. W. responded.

Undaunted, the five—Jim Elliott, Pete Fleming, Ed McCully, Nate Saint, and Roger Youderian—put up a rough clinic. "You have to help us," they said. So to take charge, C. W. sent down Dr. Ev Fuller from Quito's *Hospital Vozandes*, as Rimmer Hospital quickly became known to the nationals.

Jones then appealed to Theodore Epp who had been airing Back to the Bible over HCJB. "Will you help us finish the jungle clinic these young men began?" Thus Back to the Bible funds poured in, and Theodore Epp came down to dedicate "Hospital Vozandes del Oriente"—Voice of the Andes Hospital for the East—as a tribute to Epp's father.

"God keep our medical staff first to be missionaries— witnesses to the compassion of the Christian gospel—and then doctors and nurses," has been Jones's constant prayer. "Otherwise we lose the whole reason for the medical arm."

In January 1956, when these five young men were massacred by the Aucas on a Curaray River beach, HCJB coordinated the search operation, arranging with the U.S. Army to fly in a search squad and helicopter from Panama. Abe Van Der Puy was their man on site; C. W. was the anchorman in Quito, the English voice to the world. On nationwide television in the States, Clarence Jones described the slaying of the five young Americans by these Stone Age people. "Can they ever be evangelized?" he was asked. "They have a heart, and God can reach their hearts," was his reply.

Clarence and Katherine flew over the area in a little Missionary Aviation Fellowship plane. (Cutting the four to six days' walking time to thirty air-minutes, MAF was the answer to C. W.'s vision back in 1931 when he decided he must scrap the missionary aircraft idea and to seek after one thing, radio.)

"It was a great and solemn moment for me to circle the bloodied beach, and the tree under which the missionary martyrs lay buried. "Oh Lord, give us the faith to live and die like they did," Jones prayed. (Years later, Katherine and Clarence met the Auca killers who now have given their lives to Jesus Christ. "You might call it a tragedy that those five young men died," says Jones. "But the story has never died, and lives on to challenge young people today.")

The best leaders
are grown,
not grabbed.
C. W. Jones

It bothered Clarence that some of the missionaries who had felt
called of God to join the mission had changed their minds and
had left. Why had they become disenchanted? "What am I
doing to chase them away?" Again it was a time for soul-
searching.

Jones finally decided that "it was not necessarily something
wrong with us, or with them. They could be in the Lord's will in
other places than HCJB.

"We also had to face up to the fact that radio is the most
exacting of all ministries, and it is not for everyone. Radio is a
tyrannical master, because you must be married to a clock. You
can't allow yourself the luxuries of late nights because this soon
shows up in your work. You must be bright and optimistic
when you go before the microphone, or the whole world soon
knows it. Some people are not willing to enforce this discipline
on their life."

"The tendency of any fire is to go out, whether it be a huge
forest fire, a small bonfire, or our fire for the Lord. Resist that
tendency!" he would charge the missionaries. "Keep that fire
aflame! May the breath of the Holy Spirit act as bellows to cause
that fire for the Lord to flame up and burn in our lives."

Regardless of any setbacks in his personal life, or in the affairs of the mission, Clarence Jones kept going with an ever-enlarging vision. He saw TV as "God's Tool for the Task—Today" in Christian missions, and brought the first television studios to Ecuador—the first missionary TV anywhere. He saw that to ensure a reliable power supply, they would need their own hydroelectric power plant, and sparked the search for the site which was chosen thirty-five miles east along the same dirt trail over mountains that he had traveled on his first trip into Larson's jungle station.

But Jones had been shaken by the California accident. What if he had died in the wreck? Who was groomed to take his place? "In the Lord's work, someone should be prepared to move in without a ripple so God's work can go on," he firmly believes. "You must have a substitute in mind."

C. W. had another problem worrying him. Whenever he was in Quito he was plagued by chest pain, so much so that in October 1956, from Talcottville he sent a memo to the trustees: "Much as I desire to be with you for the Anniversary Week and the Annual Meeting, it seems best not to invite possible heart difficulties again due to altitude and strain." How could he run a mission in Quito if he couldn't be there a good part of the time?

He thought too of the capable young men in the mission. "If we don't let them take over, we'll lose them to someone else," he figured.

Very deliberately, C. W. began to assign more responsible tasks to certain young men he had his eye on, and then watched and listened carefully. "You look for aptitude, attitude, and action. You look for the spiritual impulse, the inward certainty of God's motivation that will carry them on in spite of all obstacles. You look for the one who is willing to work harder than anyone else and to work past others; it may seem dictatorial and they will suffer by doing it, but they will get the job done. You look for the servant, the one who won't ask anyone to do a task he is not willing to do first.

"Leadership is the ability to follow up on what you think should be done. It takes guts, tenacity, and stick-to-itiveness. It requires Discipline, Daring, and Discipleship.

"In the final analysis you ask, 'Does this man get results?'"

Bob Savage and Abe Van Der Puy, especially, surfaced as outstanding leaders. But Savage had committed himself and his family to give twenty-five years to the mission, and he intended to stick with that decision. So the mantle fell on Abe Van Der Puy.

In 1958, when Clarence Jones announced his intentions of stepping aside as president, there was dismay, naturally, then the proposal: "C. W., for some time we've been wanting you to tour the missionary radio stations of the world. We'd like you to make that trip as our president."

For their first seventeen years, HCJB had been alone in the field of missionary broadcasting; then in 1948 Far East Broadcasting came into operation, and the idea exploded until there were some seventy missionary radio stations to be visited, as well as many groups who were interested in getting into radio. As pioneers and the recognized pros in the field of missionary radio, HCJB constantly had requests for help.

C. W. already had toured several of these places in the role of chairman of the International Christian Broadcasters. On this trip, Clarence and Katherine's main mission would be to encourage and counsel those already in radio, and to stir up interest in "Radio as the New Missionary" among those who had not yet become involved. They would conduct seminars on "How to Produce Radio Programs"—how much music and what kind, how much speaking, how to develop effective grass roots programming. Katherine and Clarence would assess program schedules, and critique stations' performers.

Thus, armed with "yards of tickets," the Joneses set off for a thirteen-month junket, and the beginning of their new life as "ambassadors-at-large" for HCJB. (Once the children had left home, Katherine was always C. W.'s "beautiful traveling companion.")

As they traveled around South America, it was like homecoming week. Everywhere they were recognized and welcomed. One night, Katherine slipped into a little prayer meeting in Uruguay, and as her rich contralto voice joined in the hymns, one after another turned around and beamed. "We know that voice—you must be Katherine Jones from the Voice of the Andes!"

After swinging through South America and the Caribbean islands, back in Talcottville Kath and C. W. changed suitcases and took off within the week for Europe where they met with HCJB representatives. They crossed into Africa, on to Israel and Lebanon, then over to India and the steep ascent into the Majorie Hills for a conference of missionaries. They visited lovely Bangkok, Thailand, Cambodia, and Singapore.

In refugee-crowded Hong Kong, Clarence was intrigued with the "Rooftop Schools" which old friend Ed Carlson was involved in, and decided that "radio and TV are also rooftop evangelism, with the gospel going through the air. You don't know where it's going to stop until it hits a rooftop antenna and down it goes into the house!" C. W. also was fascinated with some of the studio arrangements—he noted the "egg cartons lining the walls for acoustics" at one station.

As they flew into Irian Jaya, "Peace Child" country, a fierce battle was going on just across the valley from the missionary's house. The Dyak people here were enchanted with C. W.'s trombone. (He took along his own mouthpiece and borrowed a trombone when he could.)

Everywhere the Joneses went, they found great interest in radio, but many missionaries could not understand how it could be used for the gospel. Clarence carried his own demonstration kit: a shortwave receiver that he would tune in to HCJB programs. In the remote highlands of New Guinea, among the beautiful mountains of Australia's west coast, Kath and Clare sat with hands clasped as they listened to "home base" from these exotic, far-away places that up until then had been only a postmark on an envelope. "What amazing things God has wrought!" they marveled. "To think that God has let us have a part in anything so wonderful!"

And again, wherever they traveled, Clarence was mightily used of God to encourage these missionaries to rethink the situation and press on in what was often a lonely battle. Freely they unburdened to him their heartaches and personal difficulties. Interestingly, the Joneses met many on the field who were there because of Paul Rader's influence.

A very special joy on this round-the-world excursion was to visit the Ecuadorian consulates; in almost every one, C. W. found former students he had taught at the Mejia Academy. "My teacher!" they would greet him with great warmth and respect.

When C.W. returned to the States, he was given a check up by Dr. Ted Anderson. Clarence was told that he should have his gall bladder removed. This eliminated a good deal of the chest pain he had experienced, but did not do away with the fibrillation brought on by the Quito altitude.

In November 1961, Clarence Jones served official notice to his colleagues "that it was time for new leadership to come into the presidency." Clarence and Katherine then launched into an enjoyable period, with C. W. often in his old role of directing Bible Conferences, first at Southern Keswick where Kath would take a 7 A.M. dip in the ocean each morning; and then at Canadian Keswick where each evening before the service they would spend a few minutes together at Lookout Point. Clarence's warm personality, his charisma, his music with Kath at the piano were always crowd-pleasers.

And here again friends noted how totally Clarence gave himself to whatever job he'd taken on. "He was always willing to speak or play at a moment's notice. Clarence can shift gears quickly, and has the ability to wear many hats at the same time," Ted Anderson noted. Many have said that his partnership with Mrs. Jones through the years has been a benediction on their lives.

As well as deputation and troubleshooting for the Mission, C. W. was often called in for special assignments. When Abe Van Der Puy's wife Dolores was dying, C. W. and Kath moved to Miami to help out. (With most of the movement of goods and personnel flying out from Miami rather than shipping from New York, the office had been moved to a fifteen-acre plantation not far from the Miami airport.)

Betty Willison recalls the day in the Miami office when the work was piled high, and in the mail came a big packet from a Bible school student, with a long rambling letter and rough notes of a thesis he was preparing. Would Dr. Jones go over it and give his suggestions? "Good grief!" Betty thought. But C. W. sat down and went through it carefully, writing a detailed response and saying he would like to see the completed work which the young student submitted. "For C. W. there were 'no problems—just opportunities.'"

And Jones had a special heart for young people. One new candidate was so excited when the last of her support was pledged that she called Jones to tell him. He shared her joy and gave her instructions for the next step in getting to Quito. It was not until she came to Miami on her way to the field that she realized that, while it had been only ten o'clock in the evening on the West Coast when she called Dr. Jones, it was one in the morning in Miami! Yet there was no indication from Jones that her call had awakened or in any way inconvenienced him.

Jones was still very much the "can-do" person. "C. W. Jones only had one gear—forward drive," associates say. "He could face and deal with any problem; just wade into it. If a job needed doing, he could always find a way, and the money for the project." For instance, in Miami the driveway badly needed paving. The cost would be $4,000. "OK," Clarence said. "Everybody dig in and find the money out of your own pocket, your church's pocket. There are almost forty of us here—let's each find $100." And they did.

It wasn't always easy for Jones to remember that he was no longer the "big boss." Once he sent off a letter with some pretty strong suggestions to Joe Springer who was then in charge of HCJB's European operations. Joe wrote back, "C. W., when you're in charge here, you can do it your way. Right now, I do it my way." Immediately Jones realized he had overstepped his position and fired back a gracious apology.

Later, the Joneses did take over the Europe office for eight months, staying in an apartment hotel in Marseille. When she visited, Nancy looked at the bare light bulbs dangling from the ceiling and the grimy window that opened smack against a dairy which clanged into operation at two-thirty each morning. "Mummy, how can you stand living in this little room day after day?" she asked. "It's all we need," Kath responded contentedly. C. W. brought her fresh flowers daily, and they enjoyed their breakfasts of hot croissants and cafe au lait.

In the grey Opel station wagon Joe Springer had left for their use, they journeyed to L'Abri and a delightful visit with the Schaeffers. "It's amazing how C. W. can read people, and see the best in them," Francis Schaeffer remarked as they sat around the big fieldstone fireplace while the young people skied.

Later that week, with Nancy's family, they visited in a missionary's home where C. W. was treated to a great delicacy— octopus pizza—"an enormous dish," Nancy recalls. "with the eyes staring up through the tentacles. Daddy was virtually speechless. He would go overboard to be polite."

On the way to the airport to see the family off, the children wanted to stop for a quick bite. They barely had sat down when C. W. announced, "It's time to go." "This was so typical of him," Nancy says.

"Relax, Dad, there's no rush," his son-in-law assured as they dipped their fondue. C. W. shrugged: "I won't say any more." Even though they drove 100 m.p.h., their plane had taxied to the end of the field by the time they dashed into the airport. "Dad's sense of timing was unbelievable," his family all agree.

In Britain for six months to help coordinate mission activities, Clarence and Katherine delighted in the warm hospitality of HCJB friends, staying in the gabled old-English cottage of Dr. Leon LeDune, who as a boy had been so glued to HCJB that his tolerant mother brought his meals to the shortwave set. They also toured Scotland with Jack and Eileen Brown, stopping at every trout stream while Jack took his flyrod from "the boot" for a few casts.

In Toronto to promote the Canadian ministries of HCJB, C. W. and Katherine often enjoyed a lunch break in High Park, taking a wicker basket packed with ham sandwiches, bananas and oranges, and a thermos of tea. Sometimes they stayed at the

Sudan Interior Mission's downtown guest home.

In a June 1965 prayer letter, Kath and Clare announced: "During HCJB week at Gull Lake in August, we hope to have our four families together for the first time in many years: The Clarks from Ecuador with their three children; the Dick Joneses from Panama, with their four; Nancy and Bob Sutherlin from Chicago, plus Steve and Bethie and Ted; and Marj and Marv Steffins, with their six from Portland."

They had a wonderful time together. C. W. played golf with the boys, and Kath went sailing—"I like really rough weather," she shouted as the dinghy heeled over in the stiff breeze. "I don't think I have strength left in my hands to water ski, though," Kath regretted. The family of Dick Jones all sang together as part of the music that week.

Before they left, C. W. gathered the eight children around and asked that they would lay their hands on him, joining in a prayer that God would keep him in the last years of his life from any involvement in sin; that he would do nothing that would bring dishonor to the Word, and the work of God.

As the last cars drove away, C. W. turned happily to Katherine. "Didn't we have a grand time! Dick finally seems to have it all together!"

I guess in my prayer
I let the Lord know,
and thus Dick,
the high expectations
I had for my boy,
the one who would
carry on my name.
C. W. Jones

For dear Dick, his only son, the years had not been easy. After Korea, he had married his college sweetheart, and returned to Wheaton to finish up a Bachelor of Music degree. Dick was a magnificent young man, a lean, athletic six foot one inch tall. As a youngster who had grown up in the mountains of Ecuador, Dick had taught climbing for the Army in Colorado. At Wheaton graduation, he was chosen to be baritone soloist for the baccalaureate service.

During those school years, Dick and Carol Jean and their little family went through a period of appalling poverty, in their love keeping it from their parents, both serving the Lord on the mission field. Dick's old feelings of failure and low self-esteem began to come back.

Perhaps he had been permanently affected by those long days at the Korean front, battle-scarred; he did have horrible nightmares. Also, Dick had been severely injured when someone fleeing from the police in a stolen car had smashed into his vehicle, collapsing a lung, and this hurt had gone undiagnosed for a long time.

Or perhaps it was the oversized image of his father. As one daughter explained, "We all have found it very difficult to have been exposed to such high excellence in our father . . . and then to have to accept that we simply are not equipped to achieve [the] same." Maybe with Dick it was a combination of these things, because he had not been able to rid himself of the sense of total inadequacy which at times seemed to overwhelm him.

During one of these particularly trying times, C. W. visited Dick at Wheaton. They had prayer together and Clarence thought everything was straightened out.

"But I guess in my prayer I let the Lord know, and thus Dick, the high expectations I had for my boy, the one who would carry on my name."

And it was too much for Dick. He decided that Carol Jean and the children would be better off without him, and the very next day, took off. Clarence found it impossible to understand how his son could walk away from the responsibilities of a beautiful family. Clarence was crushed and humiliated. He felt deeply for Carol Jean and the children.

It happened again. Dick had joined the mission and was home on furlough. He and his father had spent a great day in California together. Dick had his trombone along so they had played together and "Dick was rejoicing." The next day he was gone again.

Clarence and Katherine had to leave for a short trip overseas. When they returned, who should be on the dock to greet them but Dick!

He was having severe pains in his back, and it was then that the collapsed lung was discovered. It lifted Dick's spirits to know that there was a genuine reason for the pain he'd been experiencing; he had begun to wonder if he was becoming a psychotic. Clare and Kath got him to the Christian psychiatrist, Dr. Henry Brandt. After only two sessions Dick was a changed man, and with a few more counseling sessions, Dick returned to manage HCJB's station HOXO in Panama.

Young Jones met weekly with a group of Army and Air Force personnel for Bible study and sharing. "Dick was constantly talking about what the Lord was doing," one of the group said. "Through his inspiration I began to memorize Navigator Scriptures." On a visit to Quito, Dick shared with Kathryn Evans that the Lord had given him a zeal and a love for prayer as never before.

At HOXO he began turning many of the duties of the station over to Panamanian Christians, working side by side with them on the job. Following his Dad's example, Dick liked to pile all the station personnel into a van and head out for a picnic.

One Saturday, the rain began to pour down on their barbecue. "I'll finish cooking these hamburgers if it's the last thing I do," Dick joked, holding a big umbrella over the grill.

Driving home with the children in a blinding rainstorm, the van went into a skid, and crashed into a cement bridge abutment. Dick's son Chip suffered a broken leg, and the others were shaken up, but Dick was thrown from the van, hitting his head against the bridge.

In Chicago, at 5 A.M. Sunday morning, Nancy and Bob Sutherlin were awakened by the telephone. Clarence and Katherine were coming through from Toronto—Dick was in critical condition. There was an airline strike, but quite miraculously they managed to get out of Chicago, with Bob Sutherlin joining them.

"Mother and Dad Jones's attitude of faith made an impact that day," son-in-law Bob Sutherlin relates. "Knowing they were facing Dick's possible death, they were taking a positive note, thanking God for the good times they had had together as a family."

They arrived in Panama within twenty-four hours, but Dick never regained consciousness. A day and a half later, on July 19, 1966, Dick was caught up "at the prime of his love for the Lord."

With full honors, they buried him in a military cemetery. As Clarence and Katherine and Carol Jean stood by the grave holding the flag that had wrapped Dick, those watching were awed. "Their trust and absence of dismay or regrets was a real testimony of integrity to us."

Clarence threw himself into mission activities with unabated zeal. He had a deep wish to involve men more in missions: every church had its women's missionary society, but few had groups such as Toronto's Peoples Church "Men for God." His old friend who used to chauffeur Paul Rader about, Dwight Ferguson, had started the highly successful "Men for Missions" for the Oriental Mission Society.

"That's what we need for HCJB," C. W. concluded. "Minutemen who will promote the Voice of the Andes in their area, go to a missionary conference and put up a table for us, show movies." (And he didn't restrict this program to men; from his Salvation Army background, C. W. always has had a healthy respect for the contribution women could make, especially in the radio and medical ministries of HCJB.)

"Then we'll have to take these special reps to Ecuador and show them the work so they'll be able to promote it intelligently." Thus the popular HCJB Tours were started. Jones is in his glory as a host. He's known to be quite a practical joker. The guest sitting beside C. W. will be surprised to find a piece of spaghetti on his lapel, or he'll jump when a spoon chilled in ice water (or heated in coffee) is sneakily laid on the back of his hand. Jones got it back on one trip when Muggs Poole handed him a glass with a hole drilled in the side so that the water dribbled all down C. W.'s front. The fastidious Jones was horribly embarrassed—until he got the joke.

Jones was rejoicing that in May 1961 missionary TV had gotten off the ground. Son-in-law Bob Clark had built the studios, and now he and Marian were in charge of the TV ministry—Ecuador's first televison station and a first for the world in missionary TV. At every opportunity, C. W. was plugging TV as the "best stewardship, the most effective tool to reach the most people for every dollar spent."

Jones was also above the clouds at Papallacta in 1965 when the switch was thrown, sending icy glacial water coursing down the penstock from the dam and into the turbine. This generates two million watts of power, which then goes singing along the twenty-five miles of high-tension wires. These lines were strung by an intrepid and ingenious crew across this mountainous rooftop of the world and straight into the radio transmitting station at Pifo.

C. W.'s dream had taken ten years to fulfill—blasting out the mountain to dam the river and build the reservoir and penstock; constructing the access roads zig-zagging down the steep slopes; putting up the buildings that would house staff, and installing the hydroelectric plant which they had purchased cheap in Seattle, Washington, and shipped piece by piece along the treacherous roads. A magnificent joint project of Ecuadorians and HCJB engineers! Sixty of the Ecuadorian crew had been baptized as a result of contact made on the job. (Jones was constantly pushing for optimum use of nationals, and for better training for national church leaders.)

In 1967, four 100,000-watt transmitters were unloaded from the bellies of a giant Hercules aircraft and a DC-8, and the 68,000 pounds were transported by fourteen trucks to Pifo. Quite a change from the 6,400 pounds Jones had brought with him for that first monumental station in 1931!

HCJB then could broadcast with a combined 570,000 watts of power. "Good, good, good," Jones said. "Now let's add another 500,000 watts!

"As never before, there's a battle for the airwaves. There are more than 400 million shortwave receivers in the world, twenty-six million in Russia alone. Giant transmitters all over this globe are crowding the bands with their propaganda. Are we to let them drown out the gospel of Jesus Christ?

"We'll never win the war with one gun," he'd challenge board meetings. "We must get a whole barrage up there!" Even though he no longer had a vote on the board, it was still C. W. who sparked the new ideas. "Jones is a one-man 'think-tank'" colleagues marvel. "He has a machine-gun delivery. The ideas come out so fast, whether the material is technical, doctrinal, or management. He's decisive and incisive, with the ability to cut through a clutter of suggestions and diverse opinions, to summarize and pull them all together into a viable plan."

A favorite verse still is Isaiah 43:19: "Behold, I will do a *new* thing." "C. W. has a tremendously modern, up-to-date view, particularly in the mass-media field where he undoubtedly is a top specialist, and has kept abreast of new developments and technology," one board member shared. "He has recognized the winds of change, but they did not blow C. W. off target; rather he used them to fill his sails and kept going towards an even larger goal."

There is something in his distinctive carriage and bearing that commands attention. When he speaks, people listen. And his enthusiasm is contagious. "He's a tireless worker, with a restless spirit to get on with the job. C. W. cannot abide trivia. He'll shop around for a transmitter, but not for a new sink. 'Just go buy it,' he'll say. Consequently in his days as president, there were times when the board got off into petty details and C. W. would just close the meeting peremptorily and walk out."

As a master communicator, Jones continued to send out enthusiastic and effective prayer letters. "You'd never toss anything from Jones into the wastebasket unread," one supporter said. "Each communication was different. Often they'd enclose a small treasure from Ecuador, a tiny silver charm or carved head; a copy of the Ecuadorian national anthem or a small song book; a calendar of beautiful Ecuadorian scenes. And they were always full of intriguing news that transported you to the mountains and jungles with them."

Thus, in 1974 Jones was describing the proposed new transmitter as "Operation Leap." "By my God I have *leaped over a wall*," he quoted from Psalm 18:29. "With this increase in power, our Russian Division will leap over the 'Wall of the Iron Curtain' with a stronger, clearer message of the gospel."

The year 1975 seemed to have been a very special one for Clarence and Katherine, one loaded with honors, triumphs, and trials. It was back in May 1949 when for the first time Clarence Jones's contribution was publicly recognized by the Christian community in the awarding of a Doctorate of Laws by John Brown University. "This was very useful in the Latin American society where education is held in such high esteem," Jones says. But he admits he's always been a little embarrassed by the title "Doctor." "I'm concerned that I don't deceive in any way. When people hear me called 'Dr. Jones,' they think that I'm a medical doctor, and I'm not. This bothers me. Sometimes

I'm uncomfortable about it," Jones said frankly.

Then in 1957, Jones was chosen "Alumnus of the Year" by Moody Bible Institute. But the recognition he cherished most was awarded in January 1975 at the thirty-second annual convention of National Religious Broadcasters in Washington, D.C. when Clarence Wesley Jones, as "*The Pioneer Missionary Radio Statesman*," became the first inductee into the "Religious Broadcasting Hall of Fame."

At the same time, "The Clarence Jones Lectureship in Christian Communications" was established at Wheaton College—the first Chair of Missionary Radio anywhere.

Give me
this mountain.
C. W. Jones

Four weeks after the NRB Hall of Fame induction, Clarence and Katherine were in Winnipeg, Canada, with the heads of five other faith missions: Bill Tyler of the Overseas Missionary Fellowship, Gordon Houser of the Latin American Mission, Peter Stam of the African Inland Mission, John McHardy of the Oriental Missionary Society, and Ed Tomlinson of the Sudan Interior Mission. These men had made up the Missions Committee at Canadian Keswick when Jones was affiliated there, and at his suggestion they had decided to spend a month going across Canada together, presenting a unified appeal covering every world mission area.

In the bigger cities they spread out to different churches, but teamed up at the Bible colleges where their ninety-minute presentation was timed to the minute. "Some were bemused, if not confused to see six mission leaders working together happily and unselfishly to plug the other fellows' work, and together show the whole gamut of the missionary task and calling," C. W. reported.

After Vancouver, Clarence and Katherine set off on a junket they had been hoping for ever since their 1959 round-the-world tour of missionary radio. They had not seen Alaska's five stations, so with a small bequest that had come to Katherine, they sailed north by ferry from Seattle. Clarence was asked to bring a brief meditation for the Easter service celebrated on board with the fifty passengers. Music was provided by a Christian motel manager. "Did you ever sing 'Up from the Grave He Arose' to the accompaniment of a musical saw pitched too high?" C. W. asks. From Anchorage, they flew to Nome where the ice was forming a bridge across the Bering Strait to Russia.

Again they held seminars with the staff, discussing here particularly the blessings of radio behind the Iron Curtain. "Gospel broadcasts are our lifeline, *the gift of God from heaven*," Russian believers had told Peter Deyneka of the Slavic Gospel Mission as he traveled inside the Soviet Union. They spoke of countless conversions brought about entirely through listening to radio, such as the three Red Army officers posted to a remote base in Siberia who, as they played with their shortwave set in the long, cold winter, stumbled across the Russian language gospel programs. Night after night they listened. A few months later, the congregation of a little Siberian church was startled when these three young men walked into their service. They had traveled a great distance. "We have come to know the Lord through the shortwave radio, and now we wish to fellowship with you."

"We feel God invented radio just for us," the Russian Christians say.

Clarence Jones agrees totally. "There is a genius of broadcasting that fits Scripture beautifully. When Psalm 19 talks of the heavens declaring the glory of God, 'Their line is gone out through all the earth, and their words to the end of the world, ' this is radio the Psalmist is talking about. I believe radio was in the mind of God from the very beginning."

During their two weeks in Alaska, Clarence went on a tour of the Valdez pipeline. They feasted on caribou, moose, reindeer, mountain goat, and "sourdough bread, which makes us initiates to Alaska," Clarence reported.

On the back of their itinerary, C. W. kept a record of all who extended hospitality and gifts, even the names and addresses of the pilots he flew with and their type of aircraft, in a tiny, very meticulous script. "The Joneses collect people," a lifelong friend remarked.

In this far north land of the ice and snow, they were delighted to receive greetings from HCJB over shortwave radio. At each station they held meetings with the staff and were interviewed on radio. "I'd rather do that than preach," Jones says. "I like to leave the preaching to experts. I'm just a radio man." And Katherine's forte? "Being C. W.'s wife."

For Thanksgiving that fall, Katherine invited Chet and Ruth, and Nancy's in-laws, the Sutherlin seniors. They had the usual good fun time together.

After the company had left, Clarence went in to get ready for bed. Katherine had some ironing to finish up preparatory for a trip they intended to leave on the next day, and when she came in a few moments later, Clarence was sitting rigid on the edge of the bed. She spoke to him but there was no reply. "Clare, are you teasing me?" Kath demanded. C. W. just looked straight ahead.

Kath began to realize something was seriously wrong. On the way to the hospital, Katherine thought Clare managed a yes in response to a question.

But the doctor at the hospital was not optimistic. "He's had a cerebral thrombosis with a large celebrium infarction. He's finished. Cancel all his appointments and speaking engagements."

Katherine was indignant: "This doctor doesn't know our Lord!" Immediately she notified her Christian friends, and everyone began praying.

Four months later, C. W. and Katherine set out on a "bicentennial trip" to Howard and Lillian's in California, visiting the Grand Canyon and Yellowstone Park en route. Clarence drove most of the way. At a missions conference a few months later, he spoke every night in the week and twice on the two Sundays, addressed a senior citizen luncheon, a ladies luncheon, and a special youth service. Obviously that doctor indeed did not know the God of Clarence and Katherine Jones!

In all their deputation work, the Joneses had not touched Canada's Maritime Provinces, and so the summer of 1979 was set aside for this trip. They held encouraging meetings, and at one point Clarence got playing with such gusto that he blew out the two front teeth of his denture plate!

For two glorious weeks they had Nancy and two of her children with them, and once again, just as at Puña, Clarence waded barefoot in the surf and flew kites on the beach with the children.

"Dad is doing the same things for our children that he did for his. He calls each one aside for a short visit alone, making them feel important and respected, giving them a vision of what they can do with the great ability God has given them, exposing them to the vitality and excitement of the Christian life."

As Katherine scooped Clare's favorite Swiss chocolate almond ice cream onto the plate beside his birthday cake, she leaned over and whispered with misted eyes, "I wish my husband were only forty-five so he would have that many more years to serve. The world needs his graciousness and wisdom!"

For Clarence's seventy-ninth birthday, Katherine had baked a lemon bundt cake: "I'm so glad I don't have to build a fire on the bottom and top and sides of this oven!" She rejoices in the dishwasher, the side-by-side refrigerator and freezer, the compact washer-dryer convenience of the lovely home that has been provided for them. After the accident in 1953, astute friends of the mission invested the little bit of cash left over from the insurance settlement into a property ("You'll need a place to retire some day, C.W."), and parlayed it into enough equity to buy the comfortable two-bedroom home on a golf course in Largo, near Tampa, Florida.

The house is a gallery of Ecuadorian art, sent home over the years to Katherine's father and family, and the treasures of many travels. A replica of that first carbon mike sits on an end table. On the walls of the bedroom hang two of the treasured paintings Clarence made for Katherine in their courtship days—

a "Heart of my Heart" greeting set in woods and cascading waterfalls.

A piano and organ stand back to back, with C. W.'s trombone case close by. Kath and Clare enjoy the period furniture and the fine Spode china and crystal that Ruth and Chet sent over when they moved into a smaller place.

Precision and order are evident everywhere. The blinds are exactly pitched; no towel hangs askew, and the basin is wiped clean after every using. Each inch of the house is in constant order. You wouldn't know anyone lives here except for the toss of magazines on the coffee table: *Time, Travel, National Geographic, Reader's Digest, Saturday Evening Post, McCall's*; and the neat stack of books and papers on Clare's and Kath's desks. (Her favorite *Prevention* magazine is always close to the top of the pile.)

On the kitchen bulletin board, a map of the world's trouble spots is tacked up beside the map of Ecuador. And in the garage, there's a bicycle-built-for-two which gets regular use.

Both Clarence and Katherine thoroughly enjoy their retirement. Before eight each morning, Katherine is curled up on the chaise lounge in their Florida room, reading her Scripture portion for the day (she reads through the Bible each year from a different translation), breaking off in time to telephone one of the girls while the low rates are in effect. "It's so wonderful to be close to the family after all the years we've been apart. And it's cheaper to call than to take them to lunch," Kath rationalizes.

"Good morning, my love." Clarence greets Katherine as he begins to check the clocks. (The house is full of them, including the grandfather clock that traveled with them to Quito.) In the yard he fills the bird feeder, chasing away a thieving squirrel. "Begone, old fellow," he scolds good-naturedly, waving a rolled-up newspaper.

C. W. welcomes each day with a sense of wonder as he tears off another sheet of the calendar. (A monthly calendar is also stuck on the car dashboard with the days carefully stroked off.) "There's not only strength for the day and bright hope for tomorrow—there's excitement too!" C. W. enthuses. Each evening, he marvels at the Lord's goodness throughout the day. "Good! Good! Good!" C. W. exclaims.

Clarence never helped in the kitchen before, but now in retirement he enjoys the little tasks, the routines of setting the table, putting ice in the water glasses, preparing the grapefruits, washing up after breakfast and lunch.

Clare still waits to pull out Kath's chair before she sits down for the meal, and delivers a tender pat on her shoulder. There's a thoughtfulness, an anticipating of each other's needs. And a deep wish to please—after breakfast, Katherine might slip away to change her dress so as to match the outfit Clarence has chosen for the day. There is still obvious loving and pleasure in each other.

Hands are still clasped around the table for grace; the Daily Light is still read; and then, in great detail, loved ones are brought before their heavenly Father. There is grieving when grandchildren lose their way, and rejoicing when they are brought home.

Katherine is still a gourmet cook. It baffles the girls how their mother can put a fine meal together so effortlessly. Suppers are on TV tables so Clare and Kath can watch the news, close to two hours of it. In the Jones' house, everything stops for the news—and the "Waltons." Football too—C. W. will stay up past midnight to watch a game.

Clarence is still the enthusiastic encourager. At the community Bible study they started, he shares in a new believer's excited spiritual discovery of a truth that C. W. has preached for fifty years. To the neighbor who is falteringly learning to play the organ, he says, "Splendid! You're doing just fine."

But the best part of retirement for Jones is the time he and Kath have for family and friends. "Call me when your plane lands—let me know what the doctor says," Katherine says to an HCJB staffer on sick leave. So many remark about their incredible memories, their caring, and that, even after only one meeting, months later Clare and Kath can ask for every member of a family by name. Clarence and Katherine carry in their hearts this vast host of friends, and all of their large family. And they won't let any of them go.

C. W. doesn't get churned up anymore about Kath's tardiness. "I've come to recognize the opposite ends of time. Scripture always has a counterpart; there's not just quickness, but patience as well. I've had to work at being patient."

Jones confessed that all his life he has battled the same problem that plagued his father: "In a moment I can flare up into an angry temper, and this failing, this imperfection in a personality makes me ever dependent on the Lord. Anger is part of the flesh, and the Holy Spirit must help us overcome it. As he does, we take a step higher.

"I have always been looking up, even in the darkest days. My challenge, my personal goal, has been to climb the mountain. And I am not through with it yet. I've always prayed that the Lord would never set me aside on the shelf, that I would never know what it meant to be a dry Christian, a river with nothing but rocks. I always wanted to be of use to the Lord. As I approached old age, I saw in Psalm 92 that a man can be flourishing, fresh, and dynamic, that you can be motivated by the Spirit and rejoicing, and still bringing forth fruit even in old age. I decided that will be me, that I can go on telling the Word and winning souls.

"We need to keep prognosticating, to keep something dynamic and motivating ever before us. 'Brighten me up,' the Psalmist prayed. Old age can be climbing, not going downhill, but going uphill. 'Give me this mountain,' Caleb prayed at the age of eighty-five. And as you climb you see another slope, another peak. There is always more climbing ahead, until we reach the place where we'll be with the Lord forever. That's what makes climbing the mountain worthwhile."

As C. W. lays out the map of another ten-week tour, this one of Europe and the British Isles, once again to encourage HCJB workers, his enthusiasm is infectious. *"In this struggle for the minds of men, the air is the last great missionary frontier."* C. W. Jones is more convinced than ever. "The trend is definitely to super power stations, and even though transistor radios now are available to virtually everyone on the globe, shortwave receivers are still in the majority with overseas listeners.

"But with more of the population shifting to the cities, TV is still the most powerful missionary tool to reach these urban masses—*God's tool for the task today.* Television has created an open door into the hearts and minds of the vast audience, a door through which we cannot only tell, but show the new life that is in Christ. I believe that the best stewardship is to use the most effective tool—television—to reach the most people—city masses. Television is the *new missionary.*

"Good spiritual logistics demand that we use *every* means available to us today to reach a lost world that desperately needs Christ.

"In this thrilling new era of satellite communication and its consequent global village, we need to produce a consciousness of the global Christian community. We must get out of our own back yard. Space evangelism requires that Christian communication agencies worldwide join voluntarily to promote the best interest of the whole cause of Christ!

"Space evangelism is the clarion challenge to the church today, the mountain still to be climbed. All we need is a dream, a hope, and faith enough to believe."

"Give me this mountain!" Clarence Wesley Jones said. And God gave him the world.

CONCLUSION

Today Clarence Jones's mountaintop ministry has become a worldwide missionary outreach. In Quito, Ecuador, with a staff of over 250 missionaries and close to 300 nationals, HCJB now broadcasts twenty-four hours a day in fifteen languages, including Spanish, Russian, German, Portugese, Japanese, Swedish, French, and Quichua. Six programs can be broadcast simultaneously. HCJB transmitters have a combined power of more than a million watts to beam a shortwave signal around the world. AM and FM programming reaches Ecuador in depth.

Many people come to Christ through the programming of HCJB. The Evangelism Department of HCJB takes the responsibility of following up these new converts, counseling them in person and through literature, and coordinating their fellowship with other Christians in their own culture. Part of the Evangelism Department is a modern, full-line Christian bookstore (also located in Quito) which supplies books, pamphlets, and records in both Spanish and English.

HCJB also conducts the Bible Institute of the Air. This radio school provides Spanish-speaking pastoral students and Christian layworkers with the kind of Bible training they cannot find or afford elsewhere. In addition, the Printing Division of HCJB publishes books, curriculum, and program schedules for HCJB use; it also prints brochures, booklets, and pamphlets for other mission organizations in Ecuador.

Health services are provided by two hospitals, one in Quito and one in Shell Mera. Both have out-patient services which would be classified as multi-trauma, acute-care facilities. These hospitals send out medical caravans to rural communities and remote villages where needy people cannot get medical care. Such "mobile clinics" also carry the Good News to these people.

HCJB is not just a radio ministry; it produces TV programs in Spanish for release in Latin America and other Spanish-speaking areas. Much of this programming is prepared on video cassettes and is in full color.

HCJB's current project, due to go into operation in 1982, is a four-million-watt hydroelectric plant which will provide abundant and economic energy for the station's large transmitters. The old hydroelectric plant produces only half that power. In the future both plants will be used and should serve HCJB well for years to come.

HCJB's ministry in Ecuador is a substantial portion of the outreach of the World Radio Missionary Fellowship, but by no means is it WRMF's only outreach. WRMF also operates radio station HOXO in Panama City, Panama, in conjunction with a national group called the Tropical Broadcasting Association. And recently, radio station WVMV in McAllen, Texas, became affiliated with WRMF; this station broadcasts gospel radio in Spanish and English along the U.S.-Mexico border. In addition, WRMF is following up the radio opportunities in Italy. One missionary couple has just been dispatched there, and two more are soon to follow. They will work in association with Italian believers and with the Back to the Bible ministries.

In short, this is what has come of Clarence Jones's vision. It all started with a tiny, 250-watt transmitter in a sheepshed on a mountaintop. That frail whisper of the Andes has become a mighty shout echoing around the world. And again God says to his children, "Call unto me, and I will answer thee, and shew thee great and mighty things."

DATE DUE

APR 1 5 2003			
APR 2 9 2003			

Demco, Inc. 38-293